EMBRACING CHANGE

EMBRACING CHANGE

Transforming Life's Challenges
with
Courage and Grace

David Malin

Beaufort Books
New York

Library of Congress Cataloging-in-Publication Data

Embracing change : transforming life's challenges with courage and grace /
David Malin. — 1st ed.
p. cm.
ISBN 978-0-8253-0544-3 (alk. paper)
1. Change (Psychology) 2. Self-actualization (Psychology)
3. Conduct of life. I. Title.

BF637.C4M295 2007
158--dc22
2006101349

Published in the United States by Beaufort Books, New York
www.beaufortbooks.com
Distributed by Midpoint Trade Books
www.midpointtradebooks.com

2 4 6 8 10 9 7 5 3 1

Printed in the United States of America

I dedicate this book to every patient, client, and student I have had the honor to work with during my thirty years of practicing and teaching. I thank each of you for what you have taught me.

I offer a special thanks to my father for inspiring me with his lifelong passion for writing. May I honor him as he celebrates his 90th birthday with the release of this book.

Foreword

For any of you fortunate souls who have been guided to this book, *Embracing Change*, you are in for a truly wonderful adventure. David Malin has written a book that is filled with insightful and easy to understand methods to change our lives and our world. This book is both humorous and amazingly practical. Rather than merely discuss concepts about how to change our circumstances or to heal ourselves, David gives easy-to-follow advice and real steps that can help us become our authentic, healthy selves so we can truly live our potential. The level of success and happiness we can attain in life always reflects our inner health and state of mind. To change our outer world, we must change our inner world.

Embracing Change offers a refreshing perspective on concepts and ideas that are age-old. David takes ancient spiritual wisdom, as well as newly revealed scientific and psychological information about energy fields, consciousness, and more, and intertwines them into a book filled with down-to-earth guidance. He uses fun analogies and clear visual examples to help us understand this journey of self-discovery and transformation. The image of donning brightly colored scuba gear to dive into our own uncharted emotional waters, then swimming through discarded trash on our way to finding the hidden treasure deep within us, is a great way to understand the processes in this book.

Beginning with Chapter 1: *Knowing Ourself*, David helps us recognize who we have become, why we think and behave the way we do, and how our thinking and perceptions are shaping our lives. In a friendly and easy to understand language, he puts forth thought-provoking questions and ideas to help us challenge our old patterns and learn to embrace change in our lives.

David clearly describes the different qualities of the physical, emotional, mental, and spiritual bodies, and reveals why learning to balance each of them is vitally important to our happiness and well-being. If we are to be truly healthy and whole, each of these four bodies needs to be tended to. Especially entertaining are his descriptions in Chapter 10: *Intention*, of the dialogue that takes place among the four bodies, how they can create conflict and competition among them and therefore prevent us from manifesting what we want. David also reveals simple steps we can take to solve our inner struggles and remedy the imbalances.

Embracing Change helps us see ourselves more clearly and understand our potential, as well as the fears and habits that may be standing in the way of realizing that potential. David Malin's heartfelt desire to contribute to the individual's and the world's inner and outer healing is obvious. He shows how each of us, by becoming strong and healthy inside, can help to create a healthy world. *Embracing Change* gives us valuable tools to assist with both our personal and global transformation.

Pamala Oslie, author of *Love Colors,*
Life Colors, and *Make Your Dreams Come True*

Introduction
On utilizing this book

Some books are read for entertainment. This is not such a book. Although it is interspersed with some clever wit and a few laughs here and there to keep us entertained, we would be much better off reading a good novel or a comic book if entertainment is our goal. Our current culture has many a venue for entertainment, but not so for self-reflection, an important requirement for both self-healing and for learning to embrace change. This book is on one level meant to be a short and easy read that simply provokes our thoughts, feelings, and self-reflection process by merely reading the words and embracing some of the concepts presented. At the very least, it is intended to plant a few seeds. May these seeds germinate and grow over time, with the help of some additional fertilizer from other sources and from our own individual life experiences, to one day bear fruit for us!

On another level this book is designed to be used as

a workbook, so that we may become more active in our own self-exploration and self-healing process. However, the word "work" does not always have good connotations for many of us. If this is the case, then we can simply call it a "playbook."

In either case, those of us who like to keep a diary or journal, take notes, underline or highlight what we read, or simply doodle in the margin, will be in "note-taking (or doodling) heaven" when we read this. There are even a few pages at the end of this book that are left blank for more extensive notes. However if we were one of those as a child that was chastised or punished for even thinking about writing in a book, much less scribbling in one, we can then consider this an opportunity to get over that prohibition. For this book is asking us, actually begging us, to get down and start marking it up as an aid to digging deeper into some of our hidden treasures within.

The chapters are intentionally short, with each being an easy twenty- to thirty-minute read, that is, if we don't become sidetracked by jotting down some notes, underlining, or even creatively doodling as we go. Since each chapter is designed to stimulate our thoughts and feelings on specific issues, we are encouraged to put the book down from time to time. Even if we are in mid-sentence, we may need to diverge from reading to follow our own thoughts or feelings that were just provoked by the text. This can be a very important part of our self-healing process. The chapters are also short to encourage a reread from time to time. For even though they are each progressively built upon one another, once we have done the initial read of the whole book, we could pick any chapter we want to go back to and hopefully glean more from the second or third reading. And this can be without requiring any great time commitment to do so.

By writing our notes or highlighting in different colored ink or highlights, we can more easily keep track of our own shifts or changes over the years, should we do a reread of all or part during a different stage in our life. We may even want to date an entry like we would with a diary. Or we could index the color of our ink or highlighter to reflect the date of that particular reading. Thus, like a diary, when we reread a section perhaps years later, including reading what we were stimulated to write or highlight in response at that time, we may be amazed at how we have changed from where we were then. Thus, like a journal or diary, this book can serve as a marker chronicling our own growth and development as we learn to embrace change in ours lives.

These are all simply suggestions to hopefully enhance what we may come away with after reading this book. If we happen to be the creative, inventive, or rebellious type who needs to do it our own way, we may want to draw or doodle pictures or symbols instead of using words. This book has a strong emphasis on distinguishing our four "bodies": the physical, emotional, mental, and spiritual aspects of our being. So we may want to get one of those four colored pens and, for instance, use red ink to give voice to the physical part of our being, green for our emotional, blue for our mental, and black for our spiritual.

Whatever may work best for each of us is what we need to do, as this book is designed simply to be a guide to lead us inward in our self-reflection process for our own growth and self-healing. So may we each be blessed upon our own healing path of self-discovery. *For blessed are we when we can come to truly know ourself and thus be able to gracefully embrace the many changes we may experience through life.*

EMBRACING CHANGE

1

Knowing Ourself
Distinguishing what's inside from what's outside

Let's assume that we were given a blueprint for biological perfection at the time of our "not-so immaculate" conception. Since most of us have a hard time envisioning our parents having sex, we can just call it that point in time long ago when we were conceived. That was when one of our father's more athletic or persistent sperm cells somehow made it all the way to our mother's egg. Perhaps this mighty feat was actually due to her egg's strong magnetic attraction pulling and guiding the simple sperm cell home. Or maybe our own soul/spirit was in part responsible for this act of conception, or was it the hand of a divine force or presence greater than ourself? In any case, whatever was the cause (perhaps all of the above), we may now want to know what has gone wrong since then. That is, *what has kept us from maintaining or attaining our perfection?*

Whether we look at it genetically or energetically, we were given a blueprint of opportunity for our growth and development at the time of our conception. For the vast majority of us it was a blueprint with our own unique differences, but with little to no imperfections. So what's happened? Why have we not continued along the road of perfection? What has derailed the train of our growth and development? Has it been from deficiencies, such as the lack of essential nutrients or deficiency of love and support? Has it been environmental, such as toxic exposure (allergens, drugs/chemicals) or toxic people in our lives? Has it been infectious, such as the ravaging of disease process? Or has it been from the side effects of trying to stop or prevent such disease (from surgery or reaction to medications or vaccinations)? The list could go on and on. Or again, is it from all of the above, and some?

These can be worthwhile questions for our exploration as we go along our path of self-discovery and healing. For if we can find the answers to such questions, then we may be able to get our train back on track. Or we can look at the other side of these questions, *what can we do right now in order to heal ourself*, to become more whole, to re-establish our genetic/energetic/biological blueprint for perfection? We can take all of these questions and expand their context to include our physical self, our emotional self, our mental self, and our spiritual self. For these are all parts of our being that may well need to be addressed to answer such questions. As a culture, we have a tendency to focus mostly on the physical aspect of ourself, i.e., if we don't have a bandage on or aren't using a crutch, then we must be fine. "How you doing?" "I'm fine." Yeah, right!

Mental and emotional illness can be much more debilitating than a broken bone. And it can be much more difficult to accept and acknowledge, both for ourself and for others. However when things go wrong, the physical realm is where we most often go to look for answers or for our healing. In our culture, most mental and emotional diseases are treated physically, that is, biochemically with drugs. What if we are barking up the wrong tree, and the answers are not in the physical tree but may be found by shaking the emotional tree or climbing the spiritual tree? What if the spirit is resisting being in the body for some reason, or the problem is some sort of a "spiritual realm virus"? If we are only considering the physical dimension, and the cause is not to be found there, then we are truly just beating our heads against the wrong tree.

The very first step of healing is self-awareness, knowing ourself well enough so that we can figure out what we need for our own healing. It sounds so simple, as we can often observe animals doing this quite instinctively, so why can't we? Our body does this every moment of the day on a cellular level, to the degree it is able to, or we would not be alive. Our physical body knows what we need and likewise so do our emotional, mental, and spiritual bodies. Most of us are just not used to tuning in to our body to see what it needs, on any of these levels. And the answer could be different for each of us. What someone else needs for the supposedly exact same condition may be something totally different than what we may need. For we are all unique individuals and may have very different histories and issues and thus responses to the exact same thing. When two people are equally exposed to the same contagious disease, why does one person often contract it while the other does not?

Sometimes we may need a little outside perspective to help us know ourself. This can be a good thing as long as it is from a reliable source, one we have learned to trust, not any old expert with the right initials after their name. It is always good to have several opinions, for it takes more than one brush stroke to paint a picture. Ultimately we have to know ourself well enough to trust ourself to know when someone else's opinion feels true in our heart or resonates within the core of our own being. So we have to learn to listen to ourself as well as to what others may have to say or what we may read in a book. But at the same time we must remember that just because it is written in a book, does not mean it is right for us or that it is not just a bunch of garbage. The author or any person giving advice never thinks what he/she is saying is garbage (for since it worked for them and perhaps a few others, then of course it must be true for everyone) *au contraire*. So beware as we read on!

We are usually fortunate to have that one relative or friend who most of the time gives good advice. Or we may have that one relative or friend who most of the time gives terrible advice. Both are equally valuable advisors, it's just that in one case we consider the advice and in the second case we consider doing the opposite! But again beware, for every once in a while the reliable source may be "off" and likewise the terrible advice might be just what is called for. The bottom line is to be able to trust ourself. For ultimately the buck stops here, as we need to know ourself well enough to be our own best advisor. We at least need to be the one to make the final decision or determination as to what is best for ourself. This is what it means to take responsibility for ourself. For if we don't take responsibility for ourself, we may give our power away to someone else and do something that does not feel right. Then we may end up regretting it for the rest of our life (if we live long enough to, depending on the nature of the advice). So how can we take responsibility for ourself if we don't even know ourself? *Learning to know ourself, so that we can truly trust ourself, is the very first step toward any type of healing or reclaiming of our power.*

The expression "to thy own self be true" only works if we know ourself well enough to know if we are being true to ourself. For we can be ever so clever at tricking ourself. This is another point in the case for having reliable friends, family, or whomever for advisors. "Or whomever" could conceivably include imaginary friends, other-dimensional friends or helpers, or divine guidance — perhaps the Father, Son or Holy Ghost, or

Mother Mary, Buddha, Allah, Jehovah, or one's own Divinity of choice. However, it is good for us to remember that whenever we rely heavily on such other-dimensional advice, that we potentially risk misinterpreting such input. Or we may project our own "stuff" onto the situation and thus risk becoming delusional. But if we have enough advisors whose opinions we have learned to trust and value most of the time, we then at least have someone to hold the mirror up for us. This can be a huge help for those times when we have deluded ourself.

Of course, there will always be those times when we need to do it our own way despite what anyone else tells us. On these occasions we may likely need to fall flat on our face and learn our own lessons the hard way. Yet it is also possible that this may just be the one time when we need be true to ourself *and go against what everyone is telling us.* Stepping out of the box and away from such reasonable advice may allow for some creative or innovative breakthrough that has a very successful outcome. Or maybe all of our friends and family have their own agenda when they give their advice. The point of all this — that may sound paradoxical — is that if we know ourself, trust ourself, and are connected heart and mind, then we can be our own best advisor and not become delusional. So whatever advice we are given from others we still consider (including considering its source and any ulterior motives) and then decide whether or not it resonates within our own heart. In short, *we learn to follow our own heart.*

The bottom line is to know ourself, as there is *the world within* and *the world without*. Culturally we are programmed to ignore the world within and be a blind sheep and do and look like everyone else does, with the focus being on the outside. Daily we are bombarded by the media, advertisers, and employers telling us how it is or what we need. If our focus becomes too much on such outside reality, then it will be a difficult challenge to know ourself. Traveling to other countries and experiencing other cultures is a great way to break through our own cultural programming. It is a way of going farther out of ourself in order to get back into ourself. Traveling can provide wonderful opportunities for self-reflection, especially when it goes beyond just passively watching one of the travel or discovery stations on TV (which can serve as a start).

So how do we learn to go inside and see if anyone's home? If we have followed our cultural directive of *not* going inside and getting to know ourself, then we might check inside and find a note saying "out to lunch" that may be dated many years ago. Or perhaps the note was dated more recently, during some crisis period when we thought we had to "check out." In either case, we still have the task of bringing our spirit back into our body, or at least more into our body. More on how to do this is in the chapter on *Being Grounded*.

Quiet reflective prayer, meditation, physical exercise, yoga, spending time alone, connecting to nature, etc., are some of the things we can do that may help. We may have to actively seek out some quiet time, without all the external distractions of our busy world. Interestingly many of us were punished as children with "quiet time" or with "time out" alone in our room. It is no wonder that it is a challenge for many of us to find our own quiet space when we learned at a young age to associate this with being punished!

Another cultural program that we have been given is that if we talk to ourself, we must be crazy (such great gifts we have received!). Thus we have learned not to talk to ourself in order not to be laughed at. Talking to ourself is actually a lot more acceptable than talking to other-dimensional friends or helpers, unless of course we are praying. Actually, in order to get to know ourself better we need to have more conversations with ourself. For as we process and work out the many stresses of our busy modern lives, we need to not only have frequent conversations with ourself, *but we need to listen to ourself as well.*

Ambivalence can be a good thing, for life would be pretty boring if everything was black and white and we were absolutely certain about everything we did. So when we weigh things out in our mind or heart, we are going deeper into knowing ourself and knowing more about what we think or feel about something. We live in a world where we are constantly bombarded with advertisements telling us what we should like, think, buy, and how we should feel, etc. So, after a while, we don't need to figure it out for ourself anymore because we have already been told. The power of suggestion or subliminal advertising are nice words for this, however "brain-washing" can be in some cases a more appropriate term.

So living in such a world where the media spoon-feeds reality to us (in between commercial breaks when the advertisers get their turn), quiet time or time to be alone and think and reflect on life is indeed a rare commodity. There is little balance left between the external world and the internal world. The external world has in many ways taken over. We are left with the paradox of needing to fight for our peace of mind or some quiet time to reflect (but then going to war for the sake of peace is not a new concept either). For if we do not take a stand and fight for such internal needs of our soul, the external world may lay waste to any inner sanctity that we are seeking. The world has become compressed or at least it seems as if time has. It seems as if there are less hours in the day to do all that we need to do than there used to be. Or is it that we are just trying to do too much? We have to fight back the tidal wave of this outer compression to maintain any sanctity of inner peace.

We have different options for fighting back. One is taking a week or two away from the busy demands of daily life, just "chilling" in some beautiful place as a way of finding some degree of inner balance. It may take a week of doing nothing to regain some inner ground. Whether it is at an expensive resort or in nature somewhere in the solitude of the great outdoors camping, fishing, or hiking, it doesn't matter as long as we get the needed down time (without our cell phones). For those periods of time when it seems like there is no way to get away for a week or two, then taking a three-day weekend regularly or at least a Sabbath day of rest once a week will help. At the very least, taking half a day with absolutely no demands on us once a week can be an essential ingredient for our salvation. For when we don't make the time or find some such outlet to chill or take space or quiet time just to be, we will more than likely at some point break down.

This breakdown may be physical, emotional, mental, or spiritual in nature (or a combination thereof). It could manifest through illness or injury that keeps us home in bed, or even worse by ending up in the hospital for a mandatory "break in the action." For no matter how we choose to do it, we are going to be healthier, happier, and more productive in our lives when we give ourself some time alone to smell the roses and learn some of our inner secrets. And if we go inside and find that our roses are not blooming because they are choked with weeds, then we simply must make the time to roll up our sleeves and start weeding. For it is a law of nature that, one way or another, *our outer life will come to reflect our inner state of being.* So it is essential for our health and well-being that we actively take the time and make the effort to *know thy self,* learning to distinguish what is inside from what is outside of us.

For Socrates' words of 2,500 years ago still hold true: "The unexamined life is not worth living."

2

Yin & Yang

Understanding polarity in ourself & our world

Continuing forward along the path of healing ourself from that first step of becoming more self-aware, it is helpful to have a good understanding of polarity, both within and without. We already looked at aspects of this basic polarity between what's inside of us and what's outside of us. We focused on how our inner sanctity needs to hold its ground or take a stand against the onslaught from the outside world. If we borrow concepts from the 5,000-year-old *philosophy of change* from ancient China, we can understand polarity in terms of yin and yang.

In this system, what's inside of us would be the yin and what's outside of us the yang. Yin is the passive, receiving, feminine principle of the universe, while yang is the active, giving, masculine principle of the universe. Another key aspect of the yin and yang polarity is the difference between feeling and thinking; feeling being yin and thinking being yang. We as human beings are neurologically wired to do both (at least if our brains are functioning well), but culturally we do not value these two separate functions equally. So our brains have been biased. Culturally we have learned to downplay our feelings and extol our thinking. For some the opposite may be true, being more yin (inward, feeling based) and thus swimming against the current of the cultural majority. Sometimes we can get a deeper understanding about something that is not easily making sense by checking in and seeing how we feel about it before we think any further about it. For the function of feeling may embrace aspects or qualities that do not always make sense to our logical way of thinking. So as we try to embrace some of the more subtle differences between yin and yang, it may be helpful to try to feel some of these differences instead of just thinking about them.

Yin and yang are two equal, but opposite parts of the whole. We cannot have yin without having yang, and conversely we cannot have yang without having yin. This is a particularly important point for us to remember these days: *we cannot have the masculine without the feminine*. This is much like we cannot see the bright stars in the night sky without having the void of black space existing around them. The world for the past cycle of human existence has been so polarized toward only honoring the masculine, that it has come to a point of actually dishonoring the feminine. An obvious example of this is how we have trashed and disrespected our Mother Earth. The United States, the supposed icon of democracy, existed for 150 years before women were allowed to vote, and they had to fight for this right. Today in Saudi Arabia, a monarchy, they are making strides toward democracy by having the people elect officials to certain minor municipal positions. Well, these positions are available to men only and the people who can vote are also only men, which includes male prisoners, but not women. Many of the churches of the world, including some of the larger ones of our free Western world, do not allow women in the clergy. Another example, which is perhaps harder to acknowledge for some of us, is the fact that women cannot safely walk alone in many places throughout the world. It is good for us men to know this, since we at the very least all have mothers, and perhaps sisters, daughters, and wives as well. Understanding that they are daily faced with the stark reality of not being totally safe in the world simply because they are female, can help us deepen our understanding of yin.

Whether our spirit has come to occupy a male or female body, we all have a male side as well as a female side. So as we look deeper into the differences between yin and yang, as a lens for self-awareness, we need to be particularly attentive to how we may have limited or discounted our own yin aspect within ourself. We do this usually without even being aware we are doing it, in order to fit in and feel accepted by the outside yang paradigm of reality. Limiting our access to our feelings is a primary way we have diminished our access to our inner self.

Yin is cold, while yang is hot. Yin is the moon, while yang is the sun. We are all aware that we need light and warmth from the sun, but do we know how the more allusive moon can affect us? It is a force that is so strong that it affects the tides, the female menstrual cycle, the cycles of births, as well as our inner psyches. The word "lunatic," which refers to someone who has lost his mind, has its roots in the Latin word for moon. Yin is the unconscious part of our mind, akin to the soft and diffuse shadowy light of the moon that reflects the sun. Whereas yang is the conscious part of our mind, akin to the bright and illuminating rays of the sun. We exist on the earth that sits "just so" between the sun and the moon so that both appear equal in size, as we too are effected by both. The sun's effect on us is more obvious than the moon's, which is much more subtle. Similarly, we can much more easily access our conscious minds than our unconscious or subconscious minds. However, *it is this much ignored subconscious part of our being from where much of our healing needs to come.*

Yin is dark, yang is light. Yin is chaos, yang is order. Yin is our nonlinear and creative right brain, yang is our linear and logical left brain. Yin is earth and water, yang is fire and air. Yin is art, yang is science. Yin is fuzzy, yang is sharp. Yin is timeless and out of time, yang is timely and on time. Yin is the earth below, yang is the sky above, or in the Chinese system the most basic yang and yin pair are heaven and earth, similar to the native American "Father Sky and Mother Earth."

Yin is round, yang is square. There are many gifted children slipping through the cracks of our educational system because they are simply round pegs that don't fit into the square holes of our out-dated system of education. These are the people of the future who are extremely right-brain dominant and creative (yin) and don't fit into our left-brain dominant, linear system (yang). Consequently they get bored and aren't interested in learning in traditional ways, so they are labeled as having Attention Deficit Disorder (ADD) or (Attention Deficit Disorder with Hyperactivity (ADDH) and often are given drugs to make them conform. It wasn't too long ago that left-handed children would be struck hard by the teacher with a ruler on their left hand to make them learn to be right-handed. How far have we progressed now that these right-brain children are no longer struck by a ruler to learn through pain, but instead are given Ritalin or some other drug to suppress their nonconforming right brains or yin side? *Do our children need to learn to conform or does our educational system need to reform?*

So where does this all lead us to in our own self-discovery process? We all have figured out (hopefully) that there are basic differences between men and women, *and* these differences can be looked at through the yin and yang lens. There is also a genetic flow of yin and yang passed down from parents to children that relates to birth order and not just gender. So some of us are more yin in nature regardless of whether we are male or female. And likewise, some of us are more yang in nature, also regardless of being a male or female. It can be very helpful to realize that our own basic nature may be more yin or more yang.

For example a naturally *yang* male may be less tuned in to his softer, more receptive yin side because he is both yang and male. We can say he is *double yang*, so being yin does not come easily for him. He would be the more straight-forward and guileless type — what you see is what you get. He would make a good builder, contractor, or in whatever he does, he would makes things happen and do it in a big way. On the other hand a male that is more *yin* by nature will naturally have better access to his feelings and inner sensitivities, since he is a yin male and thus has *both* yin and yang characteristics. There would be more to him than meets the eye. He would make a good architect, engineer, artist, or musician.

However as often is the case in our yang-dominant culture, yin males may try to cover up their softer and more sensitive yin characteristics by lifting weights and acting more like tough guys in order to be more accepted. Whereas the yang male may have a naturally bigger, more bold body type without having to work on it, the yin male has to work hard on having a buff body. In situations of conflict, coming up against any type of resistance, the yang male will typically try to push through the resistance. On the other hand, the yin male will try to go with the flow and give way or figure out some amenable compromise to avoid the conflict. As a result, the yin male can be a very clever and creative problem solver. We need to remember that one approach is not necessarily better and one worse; they are just different. There are times for being more passive and backing off, and times for being more active and pushing through. If we understand our basic nature, we can be better prepared for how to act or be in given situations *and not try to be something we are not.*

On the other side of the gender fence we can look at the naturally more *yin* female who is *double yin* by nature, being both yin and a female. She thus is going to be extremely sensitive, not very direct in communicating, and will avoid direct conflicts at all costs. She may be very alluring and seductive in her femininity and may be naturally more petite and refined in structure. Whereas the more *yang* by nature female will on the other hand be much more direct and forceful in her communication and will not avoid conflicts or pushing through, for this comes naturally to her. She may be yin by virtue of being a female, but being yang by nature and in a yang world where her forcefulness is supported, she can be a "real mother bear." As with the males, both can have their place, one not being better than the other; they are just different. So again the problem arises when we are not honoring our own basic nature and trying to be someone we are not. As the French would say, *viva la difference!*

The plot gets thicker when we look at relationships.

When a yang man is with a yin woman they are each so different in their very nature that they might as well speak separate languages. For instance, the *double yang* man with the *double yin* woman may see each other only as a symbol of the opposite extreme, "big tough guy with petite and sexy pretty girl" (often just a version of the knight in shining armor with the damsel in distress). But as far as really being able to connect with one another, they may as well be living on different planets. They may relate only superficially at best since they are such extreme opposites (not that opposites don't attract). Yin men with yang women stand a much better chance of relating as they each have *both* yin and yang aspects. Often this makes for better long-term friends than partners for life, as the man is still yin by nature and the woman is still yang by nature. They just do better meeting in the middle than the yang male can with the yin female.

The most compatible combination is with those who are both of the same basic nature but opposite in gender, the yin man with the yin woman or the yang man with the yang woman. They stand a much better chance of connecting on a very deep and intimate level. Of course depending on what relationship lessons we need to learn, we may have to go through various combinations before we can learn who we are, and thus, what we want in a relationship. All of this can just as easily be applied to gay or lesbian couples. For again, it is the intrinsic nature of being yin or being yang that is going to influence the relationship the most, regardless of whether it's with an opposite-sex or same-sex partner.

So with all this said, how do we know if we are more intrinsically yin or yang by nature? *There is a good chance we are yin by nature if:* we have a strong and deep need for peace and solitude from time to time (needing some space), we love to connect with nature and contemplate things of beauty including the subtleties of good food or drink, can feel and sense things that most people don't talk about, and our basic body type is more refined and smaller boned. On the other hand, *we are likely yang by nature if:* we are more fiery in temperament, like to do things, build things and make things, have a lot of "get up and go," don't mind pushing through any barriers or resistance in our way — as we actually enjoy doing this — are only interested in sitting around and talking about things as long as the conversation doesn't get too inward or go on forever (so we can get up and go back to doing something), and we are naturally bold in body and larger boned.

If we are a yin male and have put on a yang façade believing this to be more socially acceptable for a man, then we may need to scratch below this yang surface of our being to acknowledge our more basic yin nature. If we are a yang woman and have learned to hide our "yangness" believing it is not ladylike as we try to be more petite, quiet, and demure than is our basic nature, then we may need to reclaim or "own" our big and bold "mother bearness" as a yang woman. Or as a yin woman it can be similar as with yin men, where we may try to be yang and not honor our more passive yin nature that needs time alone to be calm and quiet, to go inward. Yang men rarely try to be yin, for our culture supports us being yang.

By looking at the flow of yin and yang through people and in relationships outside of ourself, we hopefully can now better recognize these qualities within our own being. Ultimately, as a whole person, which is what we are moving toward in our healing, we need to really acknowledge and accept that we have both yin and yang aspects in each of us. Even for those of us who came as yin females or as yang males and have less of the opposite polarity present, we can still learn to better understand our own bias. For this bias, which is our gift or strength in many situations, may actually be a handicap in certain circumstances when the opposite quality is needed. So over time as we learn to become more whole, we can start to develop that side that is more deficient or lacking within us. *But to begin, we need to learn to accept and acknowledge our own unique qualities* as opposed to going to the opposite first, out of lack of self-acceptance and understanding. We will look deeper at issues involving self-acceptance in the chapters: *Honoring Our Gifts* and *Our Right Place.*

So if we understand polarity, whichever side of yin and yang may be involved, we can then learn to avoid conflicts by not becoming polarized into them. If we know ourself well enough, we can tune in and say to ourself (now that we are okay with talking to ourself), "I feel like I am being triggered or pulled on in some way to engage with this person." We can then examine what part of our being is being activated or triggered in order to identify this area where we have some unfinished business. We can acknowledge that the other person, often subconsciously, is engaging us or polarizing us around this issue. So we then ask ourself if we want to "get into it" with them. Or often, just by acknowledging and looking at our part of this polarity, we can shift our stance or choose not to engage. The other person, again often subconsciously, will sense that there is no longer any "juice" here and will choose to find someone else to engage with instead. More on this in the chapter on *Getting Down & Going In.*

In yin and yang terms we could be doing a tai chi move where we have, with great yin mastery, just side-stepped an attack (again, usually just coming from the other person's subconscious psyche). Or we could choose to engage with full yang vim and vigor, jumping full-on into the fray like an alley cat. In either case we are more self-aware, and thus making a conscious choice of how we want to participate or not participate. We have checked in first and asked ourself, "Is this about me or is this just about the other person, and how do I want to engage or not engage?" We now have more self-mastery by having more self-awareness and a deeper understanding of polarization. This all translates as freedom in our lives. We can then choose to write the script we are in, versus just being unconsciously directed by a script not of our liking or our making.

3

Faith, Love & Divine Timing
Connecting to something greater than ourself

If we were to look at both a dead person lying on one bed and a live person lying on another bed, besides the obvious signs of breathing or heart beating, what would we say is the difference between the two bodies? "Well, one's alive of course!" is not sufficient answer for this pop quiz. For what makes one alive and the other not? "One's spirit is still inside the body and one's spirit has left the body," is a possible answer that works for this discussion. When we start to talk about one's spirit being present or not, we are getting into a story that can have many different versions, according to one's own spiritual inclinations or religious beliefs. So let's agree not to get into all the possible versions, and just keep it simple for the sake of discussion. Let's have a discussion that those of all religions and even agnostics can share

in. (We may have to leave out those of the atheistic per-
suasion, but alas, it is what it is.)

A common principle shared by most all religions includes believing in or having faith in a divine creator,
force, power, or supreme being(s) that is greater than
ourself. We won't even try to name this/these because
clearly we may all have different names for such. Some
of us may say it is outside of ourself and some that it is
within each of us, and many would say it is both within
and without. Most would likely agree that it is something much greater than ourself, for it has no limits, as it
fills the entire universe that it created. So how does one
come to have faith in something so much greater than
ourself that is somewhat elusive and intangible? Just like
the difference between the dead person and the live one,
it's quite obvious on one level and yet a bit cryptic on another. Following on from our yin and yang discussion,
we could say that the yin part of our being can get it or
feel it, and the yang part, the scientist in us, may be logi-
cally struggling with the concept.

The realm of spirit clearly would then fall under yin
as it is nonlinear, outside of time and space, and easier to
feel on the inside than think about on the outside. At the
same time we could argue that something as powerful as
the prime force of the universe that may have created the
entire universe, must definitely be a big powerful yang
force to be such a powerful creator full of fire and air,
being everywhere. But the water and earth elements,
which make up matter, are also part of the universe and

are clearly more yin. So if this force encompasses all, then it must include both the yin and the yang, "the whole of heaven and earth," as the ancient Chinese would say. So do we all agree that whatever this is that we choose to put our faith in, it is much greater than us as individuals, and must be both yin and yang as it encompasses all? Having the lens of yin and yang can be helpful for us being able to talk about such a subject without getting so caught up or polarized around the specifics: Whose God is better? Whose God is real? Or is it Goddess versus God or even some other name? Or is there even a God? Or if there is, then is there more than one God? And on and on. Sometimes religious arguments can sound like children fighting over their toys and then one child hits another and the next thing we know we have a holy war.

So back to our question of how do we come to have faith in something that is greater than ourself? And what is faith anyway? Obviously the vast majority of the world has faith in some divine being or another. How much of people's faith is simply religious dogma? Do we simply believe in something because we are told to believe in it by our parents, family, friends, and the church hierarchy to which we subscribe? How many people with a deep inner faith in something divine that is greater than themselves have truly connected with that divine power or force directly? Or how many have simply been persuaded by those around them to have such faith? These seem like good questions to be asking in a world where people hate, hurt, and even kill each other in the name of their Gods. Many are even quite willing to die for their beliefs. So what separates true religious passion from crazy religious zealously in the name of some supreme being?

The simple answer that we feel or know in our hearts something to be true, may be a good answer. But what about the suicide bomber who would equally claim to know in his heart that what he is about to do is the will of his divine creator? Aren't our hearts supposed to be the region where we feel love? Perhaps the suicide bomber is feeling great love and compassion for those he is about to kill? Or maybe it comes back to "to thy own self be true"? *We need to be clear within our own being and within our own heart to be able to feel or know the truth.* Again, would not the suicide bomber adamantly proclaim that he is clear within his own being and heart that he is doing the righteous thing? Perhaps, and perhaps his yang fiery passion has gone way, way out of hand to the point of crazed zealousness. He can no longer access that calm, meditative, peaceful yin center within himself where he truly knows his own heart (assuming of course that he once could). So when it comes to knowing ourself, or being self-aware, if we have a means to check in to see if we are in balance with ourself — both our yin side and our yang side — we will stand a much better chance of "to thy own self being true." This can be especially important for us in the realm of connecting to the divine.

Most people who have devoted much of their lives to truly spiritual pursuits, regardless of what religion they may follow, would likely agree that to seek and find the divine, and to truly connect to it, requires an inner tranquility or calmness of heart. Many would likely further maintain that a strong sense of love, understanding, and compassion for all of creation is a part of this. So getting back to finding faith in something greater than ourself, it seems to require a deep and very personal connection being made on an individual basis that simply cannot be programmed into us by others. For if it bypasses this critical step of internalization, "knowing thyself" with a calm, clear, and centered heart, there runs a great risk of becoming a fanatical religious zealot or being just plain deluded.

Many of those of varying religious beliefs, who in sharing some of their very personal spiritual experiences, all report having a very similar awareness. They commonly say that there was a specific point in their life when they made a real and deep connection to a spiritual source greater than themself. Such an experience was typically described as being more powerful and real for them than anything they had been taught or told by others. And it would characteristically include a very deep feeling of love and inner peace. From such a profound personal experience, they have been able to have a greater faith, or deepen their existing faith, in something that is greater than themself.

We may already be strong in our faith, we may be

just so-so with where we stand, we may have not ever really connected on a deep personal level to something greater than ourself, or we may be more agnostic, for we just don't know. Wherever on this continuum of faith we find ourself, it could be a blessing for us to create some time and space to go deeper within and become clearer in our hearts with our own connection to "That Which Is Greater Than Ourself." We could do this through prayer, meditation, communing with nature, or through whatever means feels right to us, as long as we have created the time and "sacred space" for us to go inward in such a way. We may have to do this repeatedly over time before we can become centered enough to have any type of profound experience. Or it may simply be a cumulative effect of increasing our calmness of heart and clarity within, while gradually connecting deeper to "That Which Is Greater Than Ourself." In this way we allow the connection to grow stronger and stronger over time. This is one way we can increase our faith. For it works both ways, as when our faith is stronger we are then calmer and more at peace, and thus better able to connect to the love within our hearts.

Some of us have tried so hard to connect to this love within our hearts in order to have it shine to everyone else. When we do this we often can forget to truly connect with our own love for ourself. For many of us, this can be one of the most difficult lessons in life to learn. A common pitfall for many of us is that we believe we need to be loving to everyone but ourself. We can get so caught up in trying to be charitable of heart toward others, that we forget to include ourself in our charity. *We truly are not capable of loving others if we haven't first learned to love ourself.* We all too often are much harder on ourself than we are on others. Now of course this does not apply to everyone. For unfortunately there are enough individuals in the world who only look after themselves and don't seem to care too much about anyone or anything else. But here we are talking about those of us who are so busy looking out for everyone else that we forget to look out for ourself.

Ultimately when we spend all our energy taking care of others, we have none left for ourself and we then become depleted and resentful. If we reach this stage, we often have become so run-down that we become sick and are not able to be of help to anyone. In fact, we may now need others to help take care of us, which is the opposite of what we set out to do. It is interesting to see with those of us who have been caught up in this type of pattern, how when we try to step out of it everyone else screams that we are being selfish. There is a world of difference between being selfish and simply taking care of our basic needs so we can stay healthy.

But when we have always put others before us and have become the proverbial "doormat," then others often get very upset when their doormat, who they have always taken for granted, is no longer there to wipe their feet on. Mothers often fall into this pattern with their children. This occurs when the children have grown up enough to pitch in and help out, but don't as long as "supermom" is there to take care of everything for them. This pattern often extends beyond just the children to include the spouse and other relatives and friends, which can then make it even harder to break away from. Ultimately when we are happy and in balance with ourself and connected to our own heart, we are going to naturally radiate this love out to our world. We will have more to give and others will enjoy being around us. For nobody appreciates a martyr, not even to wipe one's feet on.

So as we go deeper within ourself and connect stronger to our faith in "That Which Is Greater Than Ourself," we also can better connect to all the love we have in our hearts. *It is from this love within us that all healing comes.* Some of us may want to know why are we bothering to do this, for it sounds like it is going to take time from our already busy lives to pray or meditate or go within somehow. The answer is quite simple: W*e are preparing ourself for whatever changes we may need to face in life.* There may come a time when our world gets so crazy and everything is turned all around and it's hard to tell up from down. Then we will desperately need a strong inner faith in "That Which Is Greater Than Ourself," with which we can connect in a deep and meaningful way. This will help us to find that place of inner calm and trust within our heart, from where we can know there is a divine plan or divine timing for everything. For if we have no experience in seeking this out beforehand, we may find ourself at a loss for finding any such peace or inner knowing to guide us, when our whole world is filled with chaos. This ability to connect with our inner faith can also be of daily help in our busy lives, as we learn more and more to discern the divine at work. It can help to keep us centered and connected to the greater love in our hearts and mindful of life's bigger purpose, which we could easily lose sight of otherwise.

Many of us prefer to do this in private and many prefer the support of an organized religion. As long as we can be true to ourself and make that connection, it doesn't matter how we do it. With the benefits of having the support of others that comes with organized religion also comes the risk of that particular doctrine not being totally aligned with what we personally feel in our hearts. This can create inner conflict or even suppression of our own truth, in favor of our church's truth. Or we can be too busy fully embracing the church's truth that we may not make the time or space to go in and find our own, which might not be exactly the same as the church's.

For some this may sound like heresy to question one's church's doctrines. But this is really just the same thing we discussed in the first chapter, where our own internal sanctity may need to hold off the encroachment from the outside. This is also an aspect of yin and yang being in balance with each other. For to be able to truly embrace anything we must question it from time to time, particularly at the time we decide to first embrace it. It is often the case that over time things may change either inside ourself or outside ourself since we first made our decision to embrace something, which could include religious doctrine. So we need to re-examine it every once in a while to see if there is still good alignment. In our process of questioning it and going inward in self-reflection, we may find that the inner is still very much aligned with the outer. And through this process of questioning it, our commitment to it has now grown even stronger. Or if this is not the case, the good news is that we have literally thousands of different religions to choose from. Or we may even choose "D — none of the above," as our choice may be to simply worship or connect to the divine outside of organized religion on our own. In this way we can come to find the right alignment between what feels right both within us and within our outer world. We will look further at this subject in the chapter on *Our Right Place*.

A good thing for us to remember is that all systems of beliefs can have their more limiting dogmatic side. And if we really connect well with the deeper doctrines that resonate with our inner being, then the more superficial dogma or personalities involved may not be a limiting issue for us. We may say to ourself that this is not a perfect match, but it feels right for now, and we can always re-examine our situation down the road. The point here is that we are in charge of ourself and make our own decisions in our own time, according to what feels right for us. We feel empowered to follow our heart or our inner truth and be always self-aware, as situations can and do change. When they do change then we have to ask ourself how we may or may not need to change as well. We will go more into this in the chapter on *Change & Aging*.

As our faith grows stronger over time as we work toward our inner connecting with our divine source that is greater than us, we gradually learn to trust it more and more. We learn that we may not always understand what is happening in our world around us or why it is happening. But as our connection to the divine continues to grow, we learn to trust that whatever happens has its divine purpose or timing. We often can see what that purpose may have been long after the fact, whereas we could not during the turmoil. For at the time of some situation that was difficult to accept, the best we could do was trust that there was some divine purpose to it all. It can be incredibly empowering for us to reach this degree of faith, where in the face of disaster we still can feel that inner calm and connection within our heart and with "That Which Is Greater Than Ourself."

A common experience that many who have become strong in their faith all share is to see glimpses of divine timing at work. For as we believe in miracles and trust that everything will be taken care of, it miraculously is, and often in ways that we may not always be able to fathom at the time. As we learn to ask, we also learn to receive. This in part involves the power of our *intention* (which also has a chapter devoted to it). Again, the key ingredient for coming to this point of faith, love, and trusting in divine timing, is knowing ourself and learning to connect with and trust ourself. This occurs in that place where the inside meets the outside, where yin meets yang, in our balanced heart. So as we learn to better know and embrace ourself, we are also learning to embrace the divine, and thus are better able to embrace change in life with courage and grace.

4

Being Grounded
Being here now & in our body

What does it mean to be grounded? To have our feet on the ground, as opposed to being up in the air or in the clouds? To be present within ourself versus being disassociated from ourself? To be connected with ourself instead of being disconnected or fragmented? Being here now and in our body, as opposed to being somewhere else or not present at all (even if our body is standing right here)? There is an implied reference to our spirit being present in our body with all of these possible definitions. Remember the two bodies lying on the two beds? With the dead one it was most definitely "knock, knock, nobody's home." But what about with the live one? It's quite possible that we could "knock, knock" and find somebody "only slightly home," perhaps not nearly as vacant or absent as the corpse on the next bed.

However, in comparison to somebody who is really alive, present, and fully connected in their body, we might say that some people really aren't here at all, or haven't woken up yet. Some of us have checked out or slept through most of our lives. If this applies to any of us, then it is definitely time to wake-up from our numb slumber and call our spirit back into our body.

In general, young children and infants (when they are awake) are much more present and aware than the average adult. And many seniors are really not here at all, even without all the medications. Is this then a natural progression that comes with age? Or is it one that only comes with age because we have had to learn to adapt to a world in which it is so difficult to be present? So the older we get means the more we have had to adapt by checking-out or fragmenting from ourself until very little of our spirit is left in our body? We learn from a very young age how to shut down, check out, fragment, disassociate, disconnect (or whatever term we want to use) as a coping mechanism for living in a world that doesn't support us at all in really being present. We have learned to be numb to so much in our world that it has become quite difficult to stay fully present anymore.

The truth is that our present world is one filled with much hate, fear, strife, crime, killing, war, poverty, and starvation, to mention just a few of the things that we are daily bombarded with through the media. Whatever love, caring, and compassion we have left in our world is definitely given the backseat when it comes to media coverage. The number of movies portraying hatred, disrespect for our fellow man, and acts of violence far outnumber the ones showing love, caring, and acts of compassion. It is no surprise that so many of us have felt a need to check out. The unfortunate consequence of this is that there are not a sufficient number of us still present enough to stand up and make a difference — yet. The good news is that more and more people seem to be slowly waking up, even though we have not yet come close to reaching the critical mass to see the effects. A growing number of the younger generation is refusing to buy into the prescribed reality that is being fed to us.

So what can we do to make a difference? We each must do our own work toward healing ourself that will ultimately have the effect of helping to heal our world. We can light only one candle at a time until eventually there is enough light to remove the darkness from our world. Healing ourself will allow our own vehicle, our body, to hold more of our light, which hopefully will be enough to help light up others. *The more we heal ourself and become present, allowing our spirit to fill our body again, the more surplus light we will have with which to inspire others.*

Very few people are naturally grounded or have managed to stay grounded through the process of growing up in this world. We all hopefully know at least one or two people who seem solid like a rock, or we might say are "the salt of the earth," who always seem present and solid in their being, no matter what is happening in the outer world. They often may not say much and don't seem to react to all the turbulent things going on around them, not that they are not aware of what's going on. For most of us we have to work on being grounded as it does not come naturally, like it does to this small minority. These people who are naturally grounded often have some work they do that involves working with the earth. Perhaps they are farmers, ranchers, miners, heavy equipment operators who move the earth with their equipment, or maybe they work with wood or even human feces. This is by no means saying that everyone doing this type of work is well grounded. It's just that we can find a higher percentage of people in these fields who are naturally grounded or have stayed grounded.

What does this tell us about our lifestyles? Those who are more connected to the earth, who get up with the sun and work with the earth each day, stand a much better chance of staying grounded than those of us living in our artificial, man-made world. Most native or indigenous populations who still live their lives more directly connected with the earth are more naturally grounded. There are also those of us who are grounded from time to time when our spirit, our whole being, is engaged in some high-skill level activity that involves our entire being, not just our mind. Athletes who "are on" and having a particularly good day, performance, or game could be examples of this. Very skilled marshal artists, especially ones who practice internal marshal arts, will definitely be well grounded when practicing.

So how do we know if or when we are grounded or to what degree? There is a fun little exercise we can do with a friend or family member to see how grounded we are. First we just stand naturally and have our friend stand behind us and give us a few gentle, but firm pushes from different directions, pushing different parts of our body, *without us resisting*. Then we note or pay attention to how easily we were able to hold our ground as compared to how easily we were uprooted and had to step forward or to the side to maintain our balance. Next we want to find where we stand (no pun) in the continuum of being very grounded to being not grounded at all. We can do this by visualizing being a feather or a tree, in whichever order we want, without telling our friend which one we are going to do.

So if we start as a feather, we spend a moment picturing ourself just gently floating in the breeze like a very light feather catching the different air currents and lightly floating along. Our friend, after giving us a moment to embrace this image and actually embody it, then pushes us exactly the same as we were pushed before; no gentler, no firmer, just the same. Again, we don't try to resist the pushing. We then note or pay attention to how easy or difficult it was for our friend to uproot us. We can compare this experience to our first one of just standing naturally when we were pushed without thinking of anything in particular. Next we imagine ourself being a tree. So with the embodiment of a tree, or imaging ourself as a tree, we picture it to be very big and strong with its roots going deep into the ground and its trunk being ever so solid. Then our friend, after giving us a moment to embrace this image, pushes us again with the exact same type of force as we received before. Afterward, we again note how easy or difficult it was for us to be uprooted as compared to the other two times.

Imagining ourselves as the tree was our baseline for being very grounded and in our body. The feather was obviously the opposite, representing being very ungrounded. And what we did first represents how naturally grounded we were at the time, which should fall somewhere in between the tree and the feather. If we were closer to being like the feather, we are not very grounded. If we were closer to being like the tree, then we are more naturally grounded. The degree to which we are grounded may change from time to time according to what is going on with us. It is almost impossible to be grounded when we are in some sort of state of denial about something. For example, if someone does something that makes us very upset or angry, and they say with an extra sweet smile, "I hope you are not upset or angry." And we do the typical denial thing and answer, "Oh, no, don't worry about it, I am fine with it." We are not only lying to them, we are in most cases lying to ourself as well and shoving our upset and anger down into the realm of subconscious denial. When we do this, we have cut ourself off from these emotions, suppressing them, as we consciously agree to the lie that we are fine with it. If our friend were there to give us a push at this time, we might go flying across the room with the same gentle but firm shove.

On the other hand if we are very much engaged in some activity that takes a high level of skill and concentration, and were to take a second out for our friend to push us, we would be more like the solid tree. This could be something even as simple as stacking many children's building blocks on top of one another without letting them fall. For our spirit must come more fully into our body for us to accomplish such a task. Or emotionally, if we were to stay more present with our feelings and be honest in our answer such as, "You bet I am upset, I feel really hurt and I don't feel respected!" or "I do not feel good at all about what just happened and I would like to talk about it." If our friend gave us "the push" just then, we would again be more solid like the tree, as we chose to stay present with our feelings. We kept our spirit in our body and did not check out. We also "stood our ground" not allowing ourself to be subtly manipulated out of our right to feel our own feelings by the, "I hope you are not upset or angry" — said with a sweet smile routine.

If we consider how many times a day, and thus how many times over a lifetime, we have gone into some degree of subconscious denial of how we really feel about something, it is no wonder we are so seldom grounded or fully present in our body. We learn this as young children through imitation, watching our parents say one thing and mean something else. We feel this discrepancy in the core of our being as young children because we are so sensitive when we are young, taking everything in and absorbing it like a sponge. It is the rare child who is able to keep any degree of staying present and grounded in their being with them as they grow up. It has literally been programmed out of us, *or programmed into us not to be grounded*. Like parent, like child.

Some of us are unfortunately brought up under the strong influence of *the dogma* of an organized religion, as opposed to being more influenced by *the spirit* of the core beliefs of that religion. When this is the case, we are usually more shut down in our feelings and thus much less grounded than others. In this example, we would have been told not to feel certain things, because they are bad or wrong, even if they are very real or true. Thus we become cut off from our own internal sense of what is real and have to live in the reality of denial. We consequently become much like the feather and can also become "spiritually fragile," for our true spirit, or essence, has not been allowed to come into our body with any strength. If our friend were to gently push us, we would likely not only go flying across the room, but smash into the furniture or opposite wall as well.

The religious dogma example — of being spiritually fragile — is also because our connection to the divine has no core foundation; it is not grounded. This is similar to what happens with people who live in their heads, in some abstract world of ideas and beliefs about reality that may have absolutely no connection to what is real. When we live in our head, we obviously are not in our body. Our minds and spirits have been extolled as being so much more important than our emotions and bodies, causing many of us to become totally disconnected physically and emotionally. We are then left again like the feather in the breeze or the untethered kite, totally ungrounded. For our bodies and emotions are part of our whole being. We must heal all the parts in order to become whole again. We cannot do this by focusing only on half of our being and denying the other half, in order not to feel too much inside. For if we do this we become totally disconnected. Again, culturally we have learned only to honor our yang side and dishonor our yin side, regardless of being a man or a woman. We have the expression "of being a mental genius and an emotional moron," which usually also goes with being a physical klutz as well. *We must learn to be integrated within ourself in order to heal ourself and become whole again.* We don't judge one child as being good and the other as being bad because one is a natural scholar and one is a natural athlete. So why should we do this to ourself?

Some of the more basic things we can do to become more grounded and to stay grounded include much of what we have been discussing so far as well as what we will be discussing in the other chapters. Self-awareness obviously goes hand in hand with grounding. Being self-aware helps keep us grounded, and being grounded helps us stay self-aware. Going inside and listening to our inner wisdom, heeding both our yin and yang parts of ourself, helps us to stay connected with ourself, thus staying more grounded. Getting advice from different people whom we have learned to trust also helps, especially when it resonates with and reinforces what we feel in our heart.

More specifically, connecting with the water and earth (yin) elements will help a lot to ground us. Just as lightning rods on houses are wired to the cold water pipes as a ground connection to direct such powerful surges of energy safely into the earth; we too can use water and earth to help ground us. This could include baths, showers, swimming, or just sitting and "connecting" with a large body of water such as a lake, river, or ocean. Walking barefoot on the grass (where toxic herbicides have not been sprayed lately) can be grounding, as can sitting or lying on the ground itself, preferably on nothing or at least a blanket versus a plastic tarp. In these examples we are focusing on directly connecting with the earth as our ground connection, and allowing that connection to grow in strength. Working in a garden can have similar effects as can hiking in nature or spending time in the wilderness.

There are also specific visualizations and guided imagery exercises we can do to help ground us. One very powerful one with lasting effect involves calling our own spirit back into us (or more into us). We direct it down through our core to specific regions to where it can be grounded. Again, just like the lightning rod is specifically grounded to the cold water pipe. These regions extend out from our hips, knees, feet, and out from below our feet. They each relate respectively to our physical, emotional, mental, and spiritual regions of our electromagnetic field.

With this grounding exercise we use our breath to direct our own spirit or life force to each of these four regions. We start with our hips and finish with the area below our feet, repeating several times to each of these four regions. When done we would be more like the tree if our friend were to push us again. This lasts much longer than just visualizing being a tree, which basically only lasts as long as we hold that thought of being a tree. This method will last until we "check out" again or get stuck up in our head. We will also disconnect from our "ground connection" if we go into some subconscious denial pattern, as a result of avoiding some difficult emotion. However, the more we work on staying present and grounded, the less we will slip back into this old pattern of denial and checking out. This is a very real exercise as we can feel the difference afterward and are more solid in our body. It is also nice because it does not need to involve various spiritual beliefs. For here we are not working with divine energy, just our own individual spirit or life force (that which the corpse on the next bed no longer has).

So again, the more grounded we are, the more self-aware we will be, the foundational step for healing ourself. The more of our own spirit or life force we have present or are connected to, the better we are going to be able to heal whatever is going on with us. We will then have more energy — our own energy. When the winds of change blow storms into our life, we will be better prepared to stay solid and strong within our own being, even when chaos surrounds us. Paradoxically the more grounded we are, the better we will be able to go with the flow of life. We then will become a ground or anchor for those around us as well, helping to anchor such spiritual essences as love and compassion for all of mankind. For this is something that is greatly needed on the planet, now more than ever.

5

Going with the Flow
Accepting what is & letting go of what is not

We have all experienced being stuck. That's right, being stuck in the quagmire of our life. We are not able to go with the flow of life. For that matter, nothing is flowing, we have gridlock, extreme constipation. And, no surprise, we have no energy. Why is this? What is really happening when nothing is flowing and life just does not seem to be going our way? A very common cause is that we are resisting what is. We want something to be a certain way and it is not happening. We may not admit it to ourself but we are really attached to something being a certain way, and we don't want to let go of it. We have gone down a dead-end street and boxed ourself in so tightly that we cannot even see to turn around or back up. That's the key, we cannot see what is really happening, the mud is up to our eyes.

So what is the first step we need to take? Wipe that mud right out of our eyes and take a good look around, both inside and out. Our friends are all making excuses that they are too busy to hang out anymore and our spouse or significant other seems to be avoiding contact, keeping very busy too. It must be really stinking, the garbage or whatever metaphor we want to use for that stinky stuff that's all backed up. So what do we do? We really need to stand on our head and look at the world from a different angle, reconfigure our reality. But if the mud, garbage, stinky stuff is piled so high, it may be too difficult to stand on our head and see anything, or much less breath for that matter. It's piled so high that we need help, as much as we hate to admit it. "Can't afford professional help, don't know who to go to anyway." If we are really this stuck, we may not be able to admit that it's bad enough to need professional help "as that's where the 'really messed up' go, and it's really not that bad." Our denial tapes can be so strong.

We can at least swallow our pride and go to our spouse or significant other, who probably knows us as well as anyone. After all, this is the person who has been living with us and/or putting up with our stinky stuff on a daily basis. This is the one who truly loves us or hopefully still does. We start to suspect what a challenge loving us must have become lately for anyone short of a saint. So we take a few more deep swallows, as our pride has grown big over the years, realizing that perhaps we are not so perfect as we have always liked to think we are. We somehow muster the courage to bring ourself to sit down and ask, or even plead to this special person in our life, to be painfully honest with us, no mincing words. We ask them to tell us everything they may think we need to hear, yet may not want to hear. And we promise we will listen, not interrupt or defend ourself. We will even take notes so we have it written down to refer to later. We also seek out a friend or two, who know us well enough and cares enough to give us the same painful truth, or at least their version of it. For we have finally reached the point where we have had to admit that we need to look in the mirror at ourself. We have also realized that we have become so stuck in our ways, alienating our friends and loved ones, that we now need them to hold the mirror up to our face to help us see ourself.

This is what we need to do when our eyes have become so clouded we cannot see our own situation objectively anymore. When we listen, or when we go over our notes of what was said, we finally start to take in the painful truth. We can no longer deny the truth, and somewhere inside something is growing more alive, even through all the pain and tears of our new self-realizations. For deep inside of us we know that the truth shall set us free, no matter how painful it may be. And we are so very sick of being totally stuck and having no energy to enjoy life anymore. So we pay particular attention to whatever was hardest to hear or swallow, for we can be certain that that is what we need to hear the most. We may need to take some time out, time alone for a few days or a week or more, to just feel and think about it all. We may at this point agree that we could use some professional help after all. Oh well, perhaps we can even elicit a little chuckle at ourself, for we have officially admitted that we have joined the ranks of "the really messed up." And that's okay, for we are starting to feel just a little bit of life within us again, and it is a wonderful feeling. And come to think of it, those people we know who have sought professional help, don't seem all that messed up. We figure that maybe we are all not so perfect anyway and may need to help each other out from time to time.

We think this as we start to access some deep and real feelings of love and compassion in our heart that we haven't felt in a long time, or perhaps never before. That's okay, we tell ourself, better late than never. For as we experience some of these feelings of love and compassion in our heart for others, we start to feel even more alive. It feels like our heart is expanding to feel things we don't remember ever feeling before. Yes, we have found some new resolve, we are going to reclaim our life and get it back on track. Whatever this may entail, for it couldn't get much worse than it was. Yes, we were getting pretty close to being like that corpse lying on the next bed. We start to think about our friends and loved ones and how they all said they would be available to talk some more and how encouraging they were. We even start to cry a little thinking about how much they really seem to care about us.

We know we have real friends when they are willing

to be brutally honest with us when we need it or ask for it. Most of the time we are so good at holding back the truth from each other, especially if we think it is too "messy" or painful to hear. We think how we want to return the favor if they should be in need sometime, as we have a sense of wanting to help others. Now that we are realizing our situation, we realize that there are lots of people much, much worse off than we are. We make a commitment to ourself that we are going to volunteer to help those in need somehow, somewhere. Right now we know we need to start with ourself. It feels like our heart has just grown at least three sizes, and it feels great. We decide to pray as our connection to the divine suddenly feels very strong. We pray and offer our thanks for the divine presence being there for us in our hour of need and ask that we may stay connected always. The connection to the divine we feel is stronger than we have ever felt before, and it feels very calming and reassuring.

As the days go on, we start to examine and review our situation more and more clearly. We realize that we have been hanging on to something or some way of being that is no longer serving us. We feel much stronger inside and our connection to the divine still feels strong, which helps us to feel even stronger within. We realize that we really need to let go. We may need to take a few deep breaths and tell ourself that we are going to muster up the courage from deep inside, and just let go of whatever it is that we have been hanging on to that is no longer working for us. (We know exactly what it is.) We bite the bullet and begin the process of letting go. We really don't have any choice as it has become painfully obvious, even though we have not wanted to admit it. Our denial had alienated all our friends and loved ones who had no longer wanted to be around us. As we are starting to change, this too is starting to change, even though we are feeling the need for much time alone. We feel a bit like an injured wild animal that needs to crawl into a cave and be left alone to lick its wounds. We are seeing someone for counseling once a week, helping us to look inside more objectively.

In the first chapter, *Knowing Ourself*, we referred to those times when we have deluded ourself, as a time of needing friends or family to hold the mirror up for us. We just went into a more detailed scenario of what this might look like, so we may have a model in our minds. For it can be incredibly scary to suddenly realize that we need to give up something, or let go of a way of being that we have spent our whole life pursuing. If we have established a rapport with the divine and learned to trust and have faith that everything will be taken care of, we can more easily be able to let go and learn to go with the flow. So we step back and acknowledge that we obviously were not flowing at all with anything, much less the divine. Other than of course the fact that we did learn it was time to stop, change our strategy and our game plan for our life. Ultimately we did come to realize that in the big picture we were not in control in ways we would like to think we were. We may still each day need to adapt new strategies, reorient ourself or adjust our game plan, as we learn which direction to take so we don't run our ship aground again. For if we don't run aground, and things are going well both on the inside and the outside, then we must be going with the flow. If we do run aground again, well, it's back to the drawing board, "time for a new plan, Stan."

When we are feeling a little more stable and ready to go even deeper in our understanding of ourself, we can ask ourself a few poignant questions. Why were we holding on to this idea or way of being in the first place? Perhaps on some level we figured we were in control of everything or at least our own life. To some degree this can be true, if we have learned to go with the flow of life. But when our ship runs aground or we crash and burn, we have to stop to realize that it was ultimately only ourself that was behind that wheel. We cannot blame anyone else. So what went wrong? Was it our stubborn ego? Were we not paying attention to any signs along the way? Much of what our friends and loved ones shared with us we had already heard before but had refused to listen to. Why? These are some of the deeper questions we always need to ask ourself if we are going to learn from our mistakes and grow from the experience. Did we think we could do it all ourself, or did it need to be our way or no way? Had we become a bit rigid in our thinking or in our beliefs and not open to any other input? In not wanting to look at our situation from any other way, had we really set ourself up for failure?

So how do we learn to really let go? Sometimes it is as simple as stopping long enough to see that we are holding on. Again, self-awareness is the first step. For usually when we are holding on to something or a certain way of being, we don't even know it, or we don't realize that we don't have to hold on anymore. So being open to new or different input seems to be a big factor. Being open to it doesn't mean we have to do it. It just means we are aware that there is another way, and we have given a good look at this other way, and may or may not choose to go there. We are simply open to other possibilities. Sometimes it can be so difficult for us to embrace anything new or different. Again, embracing it does not necessarily mean doing it, it simply means being open to it enough to understand it, *without close-mindedly judging it as bad without even knowing anything about it.* We all do this more often than we would like to admit. Why? Because we would rather be stuck in our unexamined way of being than be open to something new or different? Are we so fearful of the unknown that we would rather just keep with what we know and what is safe, even if it kills us to do so? *The unexamined life is not worth living* or is perhaps very close to the life of the "dead one" on the next bed, who is not doing too much self-examining anymore.

So we can let go more easily when we keep ourself open to new possibilities. And we can more easily embrace those new things that might benefit us when we have let go of those old things that do not serve us anymore. If our closet or garage is full of all sorts of stuff that we don't wear or use, much less need anymore, then we don't have room for any new things that we could use. This can apply to relationships of various types as well. We only have room in our lives for so many significant people since we can't connect meaningfully with everyone. So why spend most of our precious time with those people with whom we don't connect well? We then will be less available for meeting and becoming friends with people with whom we have more to share.

This may seem cold or callous, but we all know that over the years friends come and go. We would be pretty insular if we just hung out with the same friends we had from grade school or high school. Not to say that we don't still have some close friends from the past, and these are probably treasured friends, but we have grown since then and so have our friends, and perhaps not in the same way. We all have naturally grown into and out of many different relationships over time. So holding on to some people and relationships may just be part of our being stuck. Again, it may be out of fear that we hold on to and not let go of certain relationships, being afraid we won't have anyone to replace them. We need to have faith and trust or even pray that out of six and a half billion people in the world, we will find a new friend (or two or three . . .).

This is part of going with the flow. Life is movement, life is change; when movement stops so does life. Just look at that corpse. Going with the flow is the opposite of being stuck. It also ties in with having faith and trusting that we will get what we need in life, provided we are going with the flow. Implicit to this is trusting our divine source and having faith that we will flow to where we need to go at the right time. If we have a river, stream, creek, or ocean close by, we can go and sit beside it and let it teach us about going with the flow. In a strong river current, trying to grab on or hang on tightly to something, versus letting go and floating with the current can be a fatal mistake. Some of us have not only tried to hang on to something and not go with the flow, but we have also tried to swim against the current. In some respects this can be better than being stuck because at least we are moving. However, if we want to get out of a particular current it is often best to swim sideways, working with it until we can get out of it, versus swimming against it. Since there are many currents out there, such as riptides in the ocean that may carry us out to sea, we must learn to trust our feelings in order to discriminate which currents we want to be in. For the currents are often much stronger than us and can still carry us away even if we fight against them. If we go with the flow even just partially, we won't spend all our energy fighting it and may still eventually get where we need to be. We simply need to let go and stop resisting so hard thinking we can stand against any current. Instead we can learn to trust the flow and work with the currents, having faith that we will eventually arrive where we need to be. Thus we learn to embrace life's many changes with both courage and grace.

6

Getting Down & Going In
Busting through the layers of our emotional denial

CAUTION: *Challenging Material, Proceed with Care*

We have been warmed up and primed for getting down and going in. We may need to put on our hip waders and waterproof gear in case we experience any toxic waste or an excess of that stinky stuff. Whether we like it or not, we all have some and we will need to deal with it if we truly want to heal ourself and become whole. For many of us this is a realm that we have not consciously touched before. And for some of us, we still may be under the opinion that we are perfect, or pretty close to it, and we don't have any stinky stuff. We may have done some work in the past and believe we have already dealt with it all. For those who wish to continue to hold onto such an illusion, best of luck, especially when that stinky

57

stuff hits the fan. If we believe that we don't need to go here, but still want to be open-minded to new possibilities, which we discussed in the last chapter about not judging something before we understand it, then we can read on. We can always cloak the task at hand in different language to make it more palatable. So instead of hip waders and waterproof gear to deal with our potentially toxic waste, we can put on scuba gear and do some deep-sea diving, if that helps. We can even use high-end gear that comes in all different designer colors, if that makes it any easier. We can ask Mary Poppins to give us "a spoonful of sugar to help the medicine go down."

There may be those of us who still don't like to take the medicine even with a spoonful of sugar or state-of-the-art, brightly colored scuba gear with our initials embossed in gold. We may still be a bit reticent in our excitement to dive down into the uncharted depths of our being. So let's simply call it "an adventure into self-discovery." Because truly as we deep-sea dive, we potentially can find buried treasure as well. We just might need to dig through some garbage from those floating garbage barges for which no one claims responsibility, that finally sank out of sight. Or there may be some other debris that is sitting on top of the pile that we have to go through before we can dig up our buried treasure. Where again exactly are we going to, anyway? And how long do we have to stay there? These are quite reasonable questions to ask, things we may want to know before we dive in.

*   *   *

We are going to attempt to access the realm of our emotional subconscious. This is where all those feelings we have ever had, which we did not want to experience, got shoved. Some were too scary to feel at the time, some were too painful, some were too socially unacceptable, some may have been just too strange and out of any context that made sense to us at the time, and some were leftovers. Leftovers could be like grief from the loss of a loved one, where we thought we had cried through it all, moving enough grief for several lifetimes. We thus thought we surely were all done with our grieving process. But in truth we had not finished at the point when we said "enough." We had simply shoved the rest away out of sight, into the realm of our denied emotions that became no longer consciously accessible. This is an example of believing we are in full control of our life when we actually may not be, or at least not in the way we want to think we are.

This realm is as yin as it gets; our conscious mind has great difficulty going here, because the rules are all so different. We use right-brain symbols, images, and feelings here instead of linear and logical left-brain languaging. This realm can be accessed through hypnosis, through shamanic journeying to nonordinary reality, and through some other methods as well. None of them are mainstream as our cultural mainstream is very yang — linear and logical. Typically psychotherapy or analysis does not access this nearly as well as it does the *conscious* emotions. However, our subconscious has its own logic, but it is one that cannot be understood well without stepping out of the box of our normal way of thinking. There are many people who are actually more at home in this realm than they are with the linear and logical realm. Many of the gifted children being born in recent years have good access to this realm, if it has not been programmed (or medicated) out of them. Women naturally have better access to their right brains and to this realm of the subconscious than do men. For men and women are "wired" differently, with women's brains not being as lateralized into right and left hemi-spheres. This gives women more resilience and flexibility and thus better access to their "women's intuition." However there are many women who have either been cut off from this access or have cut themselves off from it, in striving to be more like men in a man's world. There are men who naturally have good access to this realm, perhaps better than many women, but they are the exception to the rule.

So whether we are men or women with good or poor access to our emotional subconscious realm, there is still good room for improving our access. We can do this without hypnotherapy or shamanic journeying or any other method that requires help from someone trained in that type of practice. Granted we may be able to go deeper and learn more with the help of those trained to work in this realm. However, we still have great room for improving our access through working on our own. And since this is such a yin realm, those of us who are more yin by nature — whether we occupy a male or female body — will find this a little easier to do. Those of us that are more yang by nature may have to work a little harder at this, or may hopefully have a yin "diving buddy" who may be of help. So when we put on the scuba gear and dive in, we won't be disappointed if we don't get to see or feel a lot right away. As with anything of value, it takes a little practice to become good at it.

As far as answering the question of how long do we have to stay there, it is really not as much about going to a place and coming back, which can be a part of it, but it is more like changing the radio station or television channel. We normally are tuned into "extreme yang reality, conscious radio 96.7 on your dial." So now we are going to try to tune into "extreme yin reality, subconscious radio 89.2 on your dial." The signal is not nearly as strong for our yin station as it is for our yang station, as our culture mostly sponsors yang radio while yin radio is not as well funded. So we may need to go to a quiet place or to the top of a mountain where we can get better reception. Now if we have only been listening to "denial radio, 540 on your dial," we may have to get a new tuner that can first unscramble the subconscious waves before we can tune in. For our denial of this part of ourself is the biggest obstacle to accessing our subconscious emotions. We are actually talking about our mind, or our brain, when we are talking about being able to tune in or not. We are talking about parts of our brain that we are not accustomed to using, that therefore have not developed good neuropathways. Our corpus callosum is that part of our brain where yin talks to yang and yang to yin, or where our right and left brains communicate. This process of accessing our subconscious emotions is really just turning on a part of our brain or accessing and using a part that most of us are not at all familiar with using.

So let's look at the mechanism of our denial. It is as if part of our brain is not even accessible as we have a belief standing in the way, like a gatekeeper that is not letting us access the other part of our brain. The belief may be that it is too scary or painful to go there, so it is protecting us from ourself. We have become so programmed and accustomed to acting as if something is one way, when it is not. This is basic denial. When someone looks at us when we are feeling beat up and having a horrible day, and asks us caringly, "Are you okay?" And our knee-jerk response is, "Yeah, I'm fine thanks." Then we want to know why they asked us that, so we reply, "Why, do I look bad?" "Well, you just look like you're having a bad day. Are you sure you're okay?" "Yeah, I'm fine, just a little tired, that's all." "You sure?" "Yeah, I'm sure. I'm fine, really." Why do we hide the truth from each other? Do we have a need to be perfect? Or are we afraid that if we are truthful we might start to cry? For in this example, by insisting three times that we are doing fine, we are effectively shoving all the ways we

are not feeling fine down into the black hole of our emotional denial. This means that we too have become three
steps more removed from being able to access what is
really going on. We have just further empowered the
gatekeeper in our brain to block access to this emotional
area. We have just built that wall even higher between
these two parts of our brain (or we have just increased
the gaping abyss between them).

We really need to look at why we are feeling so beat
up and having such a horrible day. For if we don't, we are
then telling ourself that beat up and feeling horrible now
translates as being fine. We have just cut ourself off from
a whole realm of information that we may need to know
about us. For we may actually need to look at it if we
want to truly understand why we were feeling so horrible
and beat up in the first place. If we don't go there in present time, because "we are fine," it will be that much more
difficult to go there in future time. For such experiences
build on one another over time, and that stinky stuff gets
piled higher and higher also becoming stinkier, which of
course makes for more work excavating some day.

In fact this is already future time, as it was likely
that there was one or more interactions with other people that had already occurred earlier that day leading up
to us feeling beat up and horrible. So present time might
look like our boss (or perhaps our teacher or even parent) disrespectfully chewing us out in front of others, because he/she is having a bad day and taking it out on us.
Or perhaps it is about something that this person did or

didn't do, and in order not to own up or admit it, he/she is using us as a scapegoat. So we don't tell this person that it is not okay to talk to us this way, especially in front of others, perhaps because we don't want to lose our job (fail the class or lose our financial support).

This goes back to letting go. If our job is not one where we can be treated with any type of respect or dignity, then maybe we need to let it go and trust that we will find another job. This can be all part of the subconscious feelings that need to be brought to the surface and examined. Perhaps there is an even deeper issue, which ties into why the boss chose us versus another person. Maybe we have stamped on our forehead in subconscious language "abuse me and disrespect me for I won't stand up for myself." This might go back to years of being verbally abused by Dad while growing up, and never standing up for ourself. And even *before* that we saw Dad doing it to Mom, so we learned to subconsciously imitate Mom. For we would go up to Mom after she had just been verbally abused by Dad and ask her if she was okay and why does she put up with his abuse. And guess what she answered us? She told us, "I am fine, it's okay, don't worry about it, I'm fine really, Daddy's just having a bad day." Well, Dad more than likely wasn't just having a bad day, but rather he was having a bad life. And now years later so are we.

This may all seem like a lot to go into and process, but one way or another we have to, as we have no choice if we truly want to heal ourself. So we might as well start now, because each time we go into emotional denial we shove our feelings even deeper down and they become even harder to access. By stopping and acknowledging them and looking at the fact that we are indeed feeling beat up, horrible, or whatever, is again the first step. Awareness or self-awareness is always the first step before we can make an attempt to change something, for we have to understand it or see it first. And before we can do that we have to acknowledge that we at least feel it. It is that simple, it is just not that easy, as we have been so programmed *not* to acknowledge or experience those feelings that are unpleasant at best. This program grows stronger by being constantly reinforced by our outside world.

This is an example of what we talked about in the first chapter when we said the inside has to hold off or take a stand against the onslaught from the outside (as well as how the outside will reflect the inside). We usually don't stop and tune in to ourself and acknowledge our feelings when something is not right. For those around us may become uncomfortable and then unconsciously try to make us feel guilty for making such a big deal out of nothing. And why is that? Because if one person in a group decides to be honest with themself and their feelings, the rest can become uncomfortable, subconsciously sensing this "disturbance in the force." Why? Because unconsciously they have been investing energy in not looking at their feelings or being honest with themself. So if they were to acknowledge the truth of the situation, then they too might have to acknowledge some of their own suppressed or denied feelings. There can be so much energy invested in keeping a lid on it that when one person decides to let go of their lid, it makes it that much more difficult for the others to keep their lids on. For we all have a huge investment in not opening Pandora's box and letting out all that scary and perhaps stinky stuff that we have worked so hard at putting away. We can work so hard at it, that often we are exhausted and have no energy left for fun things. We call this depression.

If one person starts to open the box, then others will either have to follow or try to close it harder and get rid of the "bad" person who is not going with the program. Collective subconscious cover-up and denial can approach the diabolical. Subconscious bullying is another word for it. It takes a very strong-in-oneself type of individual not to submit to such subconscious bullying. The scariest aspect of this is that it can all be done unconsciously, through nonverbal and nonconscious agreement between those participating. Brainwashing can happen similarly, with unspoken and often unconscious group pressure being exerted to make an individual conform to the unspoken rules of the group. This can be part of how religious cults control their members. This type of pressuring can be a hybrid of both the conscious "joking" of verbal banter in combination with subconscious looks from "eyes that could kill" or sometimes with just a look of disappointment that effectively elicits our guilt response. The result is the same, some form of coercion that is happening without full conscious awareness on either or both sides. We often don't realize how we were bamboozled into doing something (or into *not* doing something) until after the fact, if ever.

Whenever there is a discrepancy between what is being said and what we are feeling is being said, watch out. We need to understand that most often the person is totally oblivious to this discrepancy within themself. And we too are often totally oblivious to this discrepancy within us. A common example that is not as dark as the collective bullying comes with sexual flirtation. Many of us subconsciously flirt with others without knowing we are doing it. Perhaps this comes as a result of our Puritan-based society suppressing the expression of our sexuality. Culturally it has been driven down into the realm of unconscious behavior (even though many other cultures do this quite consciously and overtly). Overt acts of flirtation can be socially unacceptable, especially for married people flirting with others. We frequently can spot this type of behavior in others, because there is such a universal charge around sexuality, it stands out on its own. We often assume that the other person is consciously flirting because it seems so obvious, whereas it may not be conscious to them at all. If they were told so, they consciously might be horrified or act insulted as they adamantly deny it. Or, it can be a hybrid between conscious and unconscious denial. In such cases addressing it usually elicits a blush, as we have a brief moment of acknowledging and recognizing what was partly unconscious now becoming fully conscious. Much embarrassment has its roots in such situations where we suddenly become aware of something that we were previously hiding in our subconscious realm. For it is always much more difficult to recognize when we are doing this ourself. And then when we do suddenly recognize it, we often think/feel "Uh oh, we are caught" and we blush.

We use "think/feel" because this is our left brain discovering our right brain across the great divide, our thinking discovering our feeling, our yang discovering our yin, or in this case our conscious discovering our subconscious. We make only minor distinction here between "sub-" and "un-," with "subconscious" being just below the surface of the conscious, and "unconscious" being much closer to the dead one over on the next bed. We can consider that when we blush with embarrassment that we have struck gold or uncovered some of that buried treasure that was sitting just below the muck. We just have to get over what we think other people, or that other person, is thinking at the moment of our embarrassment. This will free us up so we can step back and view our barely uncovered treasure from the deep. It is a beautiful thing to see the sunlight reflecting off of the water: this is the yang meeting the yin or the blush from our conscious becoming aware of our subconscious. When this happens we are making progress. Being able to take a deep breath, pat ourself on the back, or even laugh at ourself for getting down and going in is indeed progress. For when we can surface in our new designer scuba gear all stinky and covered with muck, with a piece of our buried treasure — a piece of ourself that had been buried in our deep dark subconscious, then we know we are truly healing ourself.

So let's go over diving procedure, since diving into our own stuff can be one of the most scary things we can do, especially for the first time. Just as the first time diving from a plane (with a parachute of course) is always the scariest. Or the first time jumping off the high diving board into the pool below is the most frightful time; but after we do it once we realize it can be exhilarating and we want to do it some more. In this case, the exhilaration comes from the energy we free up inside by not having to keep that lid on any more, liberating us from our depression. For when we have major emotional back-up in the subconscious level, it can truly freeze all our assets, all our energy on a very physical level. This can cause us to become depressed or be like that corpse on the next bed.

So the first step is taking a few deep breaths to just feel ourself and get centered. Next is checking that we are well grounded, and if we aren't, then doing something to become more grounded. Then we simply start paying attention to what's going on, both inside of us and outside of us. Remember, it is always easier to see someone else's subconscious emotional denial patterns than our own. For we have done that all our life; we're just now changing the focus to our own stuff and watching it in progress with more understanding. When we see it happening in others, we can ask ourself: do we do that too? *And* answer ourself honestly. As in scuba diving, the buddy system can work well with looking at our denied emotions as we can hold the mirror up for each other.

Again, the basic warning alert is when we feel a discrepancy between what is being said and what we feel is true. This warning alarm should be going off like crazy most of the time when we are listening to politicians and world leaders talking. We need to beware of not being able to hear this alarm going off when we are listening to *what we want to hear*, as our wanting to hear it can override our "this does not feel right" sensors. When we or someone else is blushing with embarrassment, we can spend some time analyzing what's really happening. The conscious mind has likely just bumped into the sub- or unconscious mind as part of the trigger for the embarrassment. So we pay attention to what each may be thinking/feeling to understand the discrepancy. Finally, we try not to take ourself and our stinky stuff so seriously. Life's too short and it's much more fun if we can learn to laugh at ourself, especially when we are diving through our own muck.

7

Saying Yes & Saying No
Setting healthy boundaries for ourself

When we were two years old, we were busy learning about our own autonomy and independence. We had recently learned how to navigate around our world on two legs versus having to remain down on all fours to get around. We were beginning to come out from behind the safety of our mother's skirt. We were starting to stand on our own, both literally and figuratively. We refer to this period of life as "the terrible twos" because as we were emerging from the sweetness of our babyhood, it appeared that we were becoming not-so-sweet little rebellious monsters. That's right, we were the original rebels, where every other word from our mouth was "No!", "Not!" or "Mine!" all punctuated with exclamation marks. Our vocabulary was still not all that big at the time, but that didn't matter for we had our favorite words. A little later "Whyyy?" was added to the list, as this was our way to question authority. We really didn't care about the answer either, as it was so much fun and empowering to make Mom or Dad stop and scratch their heads to think about how to answer us. That is when they were not answering by snapping back with, "Because I said so, that's why!" If they indulged us with a well-thought-out answer, we could simply repeat "But why?" again to keep them going. About this time, we were also learning to take charge of our own bodily functions. We were learning to say no to wearing diapers, to become more independent like the big folks.

Our becoming successful or not in finding our autonomy and independence depended much on how stressed our parents were during this period of our life. It also depended on how attached they were to our becoming potty trained. Unfortunately for all too many of us, our parents may have been either too stressed or did not understand the importance of being patient with us at this critical age. Being firm with us so we knew where our boundaries lay — what we could get away with and what we could not — and yet allowing us to safely be a terrible two-year-old. For if they engaged us at our own level and replied, "Don't you say 'no' to me!" and never let us keep what we claimed as "mine," by always taking things away from us with "that's not yours!" then we were doomed for life. We were equally doomed if they put a lot of pressure on us to become potty trained before we were ready to do it on our own (with perhaps just a little instruction and encouragement).

A word about our parents, grandparents or primary caregivers at that critical age: If we are the type that is prone to the "blame, shame, name-calling game," then we need to step back out of this polarity. For if we are prone to do this then we can be sure that we have had it done to us and did not like it, so why should we do it to others, much less our parents? In most cases our parents, or our early caregivers, were doing the best they knew how and may have been simply over their heads with stress, over whatever. There is no training or certification program to become a parent. The sperm simply has to find the egg and it's a done deal, other than the mother hoping that the father stays around long enough to help raise the child. So what good is it going to do us to hold on to blame or resentment for our parents for not having it together?

It is said that on a soul level we choose our parents in order to have a certain type of learning experience. If this is true we should be thanking them for any incompetence they may have had, causing them to fall short of being perfect as parents so we could learn. This is part of what we talked about in the letting go and going with the flow discussion. So if this is the case, why are we then so doomed? We are doomed in that we now have to go out into the world without having any healthy boundaries or knowing how to say no. For we likely are going to have to learn these lessons the hard way. The easy way was if we had come away from our early child-hood already having mastered these lessons during our terrible twos.

This was our time for learning to be autonomous and independent. And if we weren't allowed to experi-ence being either, we likely are to be walked all over by others for the rest of our life. Some of us were fortunate during our adolescence and made up for lost time. For with all the vehemence of an almost full-grown two-year-old, we would become "the rebellious teenager from hell" and learn these lessons then. With the forced potty training scenario, we learned to succumb to the pressure of doing the right thing in order to please our parents. This often was from fear of not being loved if we didn't walk the line. In this case we never got the chance to develop our own sense of self, for we learned we had to please others first.

In either case we became shortchanged in our op-portunity to learn to stand on our own, develop a good sense of self and be able to say no when we need to. We could call this story "The Early Days in the Life of a Doormat" (or of an "Open Door"). So why is this so critical? The ramifications later in life can be extensive. This age period was part of our formative years. This was when we formulated our ways to relate to the out-side world. Remember inside, yin, learning how to stand against the outside, yang. And guess what? A lot of this learning was occurring in the emotional subconscious realm. That's right, we were being programmed or imprinted by these early childhood experiences that most of us don't even remember now as adults. We don't remember because remembering things is mostly a conscious mind function. This type of learning or programming was happening more predominantly in our subconscious minds. It is also possible that our boundaries were violated in a more extreme way during this critical developmental period, such as by sexual abuse. The effects later in life are very similar if this occurred at that age, being a major violation of boundaries where our personal space was not respected, as we were not able to say no. Or perhaps we believed this was what we had to do in order to please someone to be loved, as with the forced potty training scenario.

Perhaps the biggest ramification of not being able to fully develop healthy boundaries or a strong sense of self is our immune system. For this is not just about being able to say no to other people; it can involve saying no to other invading critters as well, such as parasites (microbial or human), viruses, bacteria, fungi, etc. When we don't have healthy boundaries with people, we most always don't have good boundaries with foreign invading organisms either. Remember in the previous chapter (the one we may have had to read more than once to really get all the implications), we said that it took a rare person with a very strong sense of self to stand up to the subtle unconscious manipulations of others. It is interesting to note that those with a very poor sense or no sense of self, with an extreme deficiency in their ability to say no, can also become very manipulative. Since they don't know how to stand up for themself and say no directly, they learn to be masters of more indirect means, such as being conniving and well versed in the art of manipulation. Another reason is since they don't have boundaries around themself, they therefore are not able to recognize any boundaries around others, "what's yours is mine." This would be a more extreme case of having no boundaries or not being able to say no, however we all have experiences with people like this. The more common situation is for us to be like a doormat, being walked all over by certain people, such as those just mentioned. For if we are kind, caring, and considerate of others, we assume in our naïveté that others will be as well. It is good for us to remember that often when others are not being respectful, kind or considerate, it is because they are acting out of some unconscious program of which they are not aware.

Most of us have experienced some degree or another of this. For as mentioned, it goes back to our yin inner self having difficulty in holding off the onslaught from the yang outside. This common cultural phenomenon can be greatly exacerbated if the early development of our boundaries was short-circuited as a young child or again as a teenager. Many times we have tried to reclaim this right to say no as an adult and have failed. For it is like being a toddler taking our first steps and falling flat on our face; we simply need to get back up and try again. If we have people around us who are unconsciously used to taking advantage of our lack of boundaries, then they will likely also unconsciously resist our changing. They may subconsciously try to thwart us, or sabotage us, in our efforts to change this pattern or program. They will often employ guilt as a means to their unconscious end of preserving their doormat. We may agree with them and tell ourself, "Yes, we are being selfish for saying no or standing up for ourself" as we fall back on our face onto the floor (where doormats belong). So up we get again *and persevere, as it is better late than never to learn to say no.* So how do we go about this?

A good way to start is by using the same old formula: First we feel the discrepancy between what is being said and what we feel inside. In other words, something does not feel right or good about these types of interactions. We then stop and pay attention to our feelings. This is all a part of the self-awareness step. What are we actually feeling or experiencing? This is a right-brain, yin function, so we may have images or symbols coming to us as our answer or maybe coming to us through our dreams at night. We can write down these dreams, images, and symbols so we don't forget them. They may be as simple as an image of being strangled so we can't breath or of being stepped on or being trapped. What do they mean? We ask this as a more left-brain, yang function, to get understanding or interpretation. This is now part of the self-examination step, so we first feel and then think about what we feel. For some it could be the opposite; we first think and then feel what we are thinking about. It really doesn't matter, *as long as we do both*. Those of us who are more yang, left-brain dominant will think first because that comes more naturally. While those of us who are more yin, right-brain dominant, will feel first as that comes more naturally. Either way we have to let that sunshine reflect on the water, so both our yin and yang sides can work together in this self-awareness/self-examination stage, before we choose to act on it. Over time, with repeated experience of doing this, we then learn to trust what we are coming up with, as it is usually accurate.

As we continue on this self-awareness and self-examination process, we are trying to determine what is wrong with this picture and what we need to do about it. We may need to talk to a few friends about it (not the guilt-tripping friends hopefully, not yet anyway), perhaps friends who are more removed from the situation. If we are really stuck we could even talk with a professional counselor about it. Then we come to a point when we are finally feeling clear about the nature of our situation that involves us being able to say no and establish healthy boundaries for ourself. For we realize that it is also about *being able to say yes to ourself when we need to*. We are ready to pick ourself up off the floor and try walking on our own two feet again. This is a good time to work with being grounded. For the task now at hand is going to require us being solid within ourself, so we can express our truth to those who may not want to hear it. And we understand that it is most likely their subconscious or unconscious self that is not wanting to hear it.

So we share honestly what we have discovered about ourself, either in person or in a letter, if we think/feel it will be better heard that way. We explain that we are working on creating healthy boundaries in our life for ourself. We further let them know that we need their help, since they are so involved in our life right now. We need their help to support us in this aspect of our personal growth as we are working on breaking out of this pattern of being a doormat for everyone else. We tell them that we know that it was we who enabled them and others to walk all over us in certain situations. And that we know that this has not been anything malicious or deliberate; it's just part of the pattern we have all been participating in. However, we are now choosing not to participate in any such unhealthy patterns anymore. We let them know that we are just learning to set boundaries now, and that we may be awkward in this process at first. We ask them to please not take it personally if we have to scream "No!" "Not!" "Stop!" or "This is my space! Don't cross this line!" from time to time until we can learn to say no in a softer or more gentle way. We actually are working toward when we don't even need to say no, for our strong and healthy personal boundaries will be naturally conveyed without words. We are aware that we are swimming against the tide or currents of what has been. And because of this, we may end up on the shore at a place that is not exactly where we want to be during this learning phase.

The scariest part of this process is not knowing if these close people in our lives will be able to support our growth and change with us. Especially now that we have brought it up from the unconscious to the conscious level. For if they continue to repeatedly refuse to stay conscious with this process after many times of being reminded, then that can mean perhaps two things: We are living with or hanging out with unconscious people who refuse to become conscious around these issues that are extremely important to us. Or what is worse, but not as likely, that this person (these people in our life) is consciously choosing to disrespect us and not honor us in our growth. *Healthy boundaries means being able to choose what or whom we want to have in our life, and what or whom we do not want to have in our life.* The consequence of establishing healthy boundaries in our life, when we previously did not have any, is that some or many of the people who used to be close to us will not be allowed in anymore. For we have now established our healthy boundaries to only allow in those people who can honor and respect us as we want to be honored and respected. Therefore certain people who were previously an important part of our life, may not be able to rise to the occasion of both consciously and subconsciously honoring and respecting us. *For we have learned to respect ourself and say yes to ourself as well as to say no to those who do not respect us.* These people will no longer be allowed in to our inner circle of those whom we can trust to be honoring and respectful of us.

The beautiful part of this process, to help balance out the scary part, is that we are now available to receive new people into our new inner circle of trusted ones. This is a new position that had not previously been created, so we are now taking applications. Remember there are six and a half billion people in the world to choose from. Joking set aside, we don't need to go seeking such people. We will naturally attract them to us just as, before we established healthy personal boundaries, we attracted those people to us who did not respect boundaries. Our changes will have ramifications on not only our more intimate personal life, but also on our outer social life and on our professional life or place of work. We may in some cases find that we actually had to walk away from a relationship before the other person realized that we really meant it. However, beware, for this type of boundariless person who is so slow to wake up and change may not have really changed. They may just be saying all the right things to get us back as another form of manipulation. And yet in some cases (unfortunately rare ones) they have actually changed and learned to get with the program, as we have done them a huge favor in helping them to understand boundaries.

We will likely have transitional types of relationships, situations, or tests as we become more established in our new self, a self with more self-respect. We will attract these transitional situations or relationships that will reflect our state of transition along the continuum. This is the continuum of having no boundaries and not being able to say no, to having healthy and strong boundaries and being able to say yes or no as appropriate. Life will begin to provide us with such transitional situations and relationships that may look like the former ones where we were not being honored and respected as we wanted or needed to be. However, with these people or situations, we will have less and less problem in saying no. For they will represent a pop quiz of life to make sure we have really learned our lessons. Next we will attract more challenging ones, where we at first feel like we are being well respected and honored, at least much more so than before. But after a while we will find that even these are not fully honoring us and respecting us as we need to be or *as we know inside that we deserve to be.*

So as we progress and get stronger in ourself, in our boundaries and our ability to say yes or no, we may have a few other tests or pop quizzes along the way and then often have one last final exam on this given issue. Again these will reflect our more recent progress along the continuum. These tests see if we are now ready to really receive into our life those people and situations where we can truly be loved, honored, and respected. For we will attract such people and situations into our life only when we have truly learned to love, honor, and respect our own self. So learning how to say yes to ourself is an important part of learning to say both yes and no in our life. This is a critical part of the balance between the inside and the outside, which is a vital aspect of healing ourself and becoming more whole as we learn to more easily embrace change in our life.

8

Honoring Our Gifts
Acknowledging our unique individuality & talents

When we try to fathom what over *six and a half billion* people currently living on this planet means for us, it can be quite difficult. It can be equally as unfathomable to realize that there are no two individuals exactly alike. All six and a half billion of us may be human beings, but we all have our own unique genetic makeup. We have our own individual DNA combinations causing each of us to have specific internal and external characteristics. If we consider the idea that we, on a soul level, may have chosen our parents and the specific time to come into this world, we may then wonder why. Perhaps it was so we could be exposed to particular types of circumstances and experiences from which we could learn and develop. We may have needed certain lessons in order to develop our character or specific talents and abilities. Maybe we came to be with certain people in our life to help love and support them along their way (or them us), or for them to be our nemesis to challenge us in a big way (or us them).

In either case, if we had been born into other circumstances at another time or place, this may not have been as possible. These experiences and people may have exposed us to both specific opportunities, as well as to struggles and challenges that have helped to shape us, or forge us into who we are. Different parents would have given us other genes and thus different internal and external characteristics, other types of gifts, talents, and shortcomings, as well as a different home environment. Such other parents may not have been as helpful for us in our development or in learning what we need to learn. This can give us perspective on our parents if we are prone to blaming them for our shortcomings. For we may have chosen them on some level to be the anvil, helping to forge our growth and development.

To help understand how our experiences in life can shape us, let's consider some of the more common or shared experiences that many of us have had. The previous generations that may have possibly included our parents, grandparents, or even great-grandparents, experienced World War I, the Great Depression, and perhaps World War II. They were effected by these common experiences in ways that were different than the next generation. For example, they developed a certain relationship to scarcity during the Depression, perhaps causing them to be frugal or even hording. Our parents or grandparents may have been a part of the next generation that lived through World War II, the Korean War, the Cold War, and the war in Vietnam. A certain relationship to freedom and fear may have been part of their group consciousness. We may have lived through one or two of these more recent wars, plus two wars in the Middle East, 9/11, and now in a period of mass *globalization*. We may want to look at how these shared experiences have affected us. For Americans, 9/11 has greatly influenced many of us in regard to our relationship to fear. Our group sense of safety and security was obviously affected in that it was the only time that one of our major cities has been attacked and without apparent warning. These are just a few examples of key things that have greatly influenced and shaped our collective reality over the last few generations. They are hallmarks on our *mass* consciousness, while at the same time we each have had many personal experiences, including trauma and success, hallmark our *individual* consciousness.

So we are looking in the back door to see some of the different aspects of nature versus nurture in our lives. We are noticing how we all differ and have been shaped by our own nature, be it yin or yang, or due to our individual genetic makeup versus our outer world experiences, both personal and cultural. The result is the same whether it is coming from the cards we were dealt in our hand of life, or from how we have played our cards. Or perhaps for some of us how we have been played in the game of life. We are each unique from both our internal makeup and from our external experiences that have shaped us.

We might ask why are we bothering to look at this anyway? This is part of seeing the big picture, for as we can better see this in our life, we can better know ourself. Then we can better understand how we may need to embrace life's changes to become more whole or more connected with who we really are. We are simply utilizing a different dissecting tool to take us apart for a closer look. Or for those of us who have had enough talk about corpses, we are merely using another lens to look closer at ourself, for we can see only so much by holding up the mirror. We have focused so far more on the general and on our shared or collective outer world experiences. Let's now look at our more personal or individual experiences that may have shaped us.

When we apply for a loan, we would be looked at according to our personal or individual assets and liabilities. We can't simply tell the bank that our assets and debts are similar to the rest of our generation. Well, we could, but if we want to get the loan, they will want to examine our personal loan history and want our individual tax returns. So what are some of the more personal experiences that may have shaped us into who we now are? What are some of our individual assets and debts? What characteristics do we have that might be looked at as our good points and our bad points, as we specifically evaluate ourself in a more personal way?

The bank will just be looking at our financial strengths and weaknesses. Hopefully there is more to us than that. If we were being picked for a weekend softball team, the other players might want to know if we can throw the ball well, or hit it far, or are good at catching. Maybe we are good in all of these skills, but we are very overweight and thus very slow at running. This could be similar for a job interview, for our potential employer will want to know both our strengths and weaknesses. They should pertain more to the nature of the job requirements, as they likely (and hopefully) will not be asking if we are a good lover. All of this apparently superfluous discussion here has actually been to help stimulate us to start thinking. For our subconscious mind has likely already begun thinking about some of the things we may be good at or have a natural gift for, no matter how silly our conscious mind may judge them to be.

Maybe they are not silly, but are attributes that we never have considered as being gifts. For instance many people are natural teachers, patiently being able to show or explain things to others, but never have thought of themselves as being a teacher. Others may be wonderful listeners, without judging or giving advice, just being fully present and listening, for this too truly can be a gift. Possibly our best trait is having a great smile that really radiates and makes others feel good. Some people hate the fact that they so easily cry for no apparent reason.

Perhaps the world needs people to shed tears to help make up for all the unshed ones. This could be our gift to the world and we don't even know it.

The sad truth is that we are not usually supported in looking at our good traits, unless we are exceptionally good at something that is well valued. If we do focus on our talents, we are often judged as being vain or egotistical for doing so, including by ourself. As a consequence we tend to put much more focus on our weaknesses, faults, and shortcomings (unless of course we are applying for that job). We need to remember to keep a healthy balance between our yin and yang, for we can't be tearing ourself down all the time; we need to build ourself up as well. And the opposite is true for some of us; we could use less building up and more well-honed constructive criticism. The tearing down of an excessively large ego will often uncover just the opposite hiding behind it. However, most of us have been infected by the widespread cultural epidemic of poor self-esteem resulting in lack of self-confidence. So it can be a good thing to take time out and start acknowledging our assets: our gifts, talents, and skills. We can begin this inventory by simply listing them, including both those inherited traits such as a great smile, a quick and clever wit, etc., as well as those things we have developed and learned to do through many hours of practice and hard work. If we just write them down at first, like a free stream of thought without judging them, we will have better access to them, even if they may seem silly or inconsequential. Some things that we may be accustomed to looking at as a fault may actually be a gift in disguise.

This can be another way of uncovering some of our buried treasure within us. However, the process may still have to go through many layers of stinky muck to get to our treasure. This can include much of our social programming that has disconnected us from being able to honor our gifts. There may even be some pain or tears involved in this uncovering process. For example, we may believe deep inside that we have a great voice for singing, yet have had a few critical experiences where we were put down, laughed at, or otherwise told that we don't. So the uncovering process may be a recovery process of reowning or reconnecting to our gifts, as we may actually have a quite beautiful singing voice. It may not be a voice that will star up on stage behind a microphone (unless it's karaoke), but it may be a voice that can move our emotions from deep inside our being out to the surface. Even if we think that it may only directly benefit us, because we feel so much better after singing, it can indirectly be of value to both us and the world as well. For the world is going to be a better place by having even one more person better connected to their heart and soul. If our own children or others in our care, are in distress, our singing to them may make more difference in their life than we may ever know. This could simply be by rocking a baby asleep while singing to them from our heart.

*   *   *

One of the layers of muck that really stinks and keeps many of us from accessing the buried treasure of our hidden gifts is *our need to compare*. We like to compare ourself to someone else that *seems* more naturally gifted than we are in a given area. They may not be as naturally gifted as we are, but they have spent more hours of practice to become good at it. So we then turn it around on ourself, telling ourself that we could never be that good. Or worse, we may hate and resent them for having developed their gifts and becoming successful. Often in this situation we are simply projecting our own hate and resentment of ourself for not putting the time in to develop that same gift. Or we may be regretting a choice we made in life to pursue something else versus developing that particular talent. We may even think we did not have the choice and were forced to give it up, perhaps in order to have a family instead. We need to remember that we always have choice, even when we think we don't, and not play the victim role and be resentful.

These are all examples of how that muck might really smell once we decide to do some digging. We may need to be really honest with ourself in order to sort through it all to get to the truth that can lead us to our treasures. It is also helpful for us to remember that many of us have similar gifts. Therefore there will most always be those who are better than us, as well as those who have not developed that gift as well as we have. And if there is nobody else currently as good as we are at something, then we just need to wait, for someday there will come someone who is better than we are. And we may never know it, but it may have been us who inspired them to be their very best.

So for those of us who are still scratching our heads trying to think of something at which we are good or gifted, we may have to think about what we loved to do as a child. We may have been exposed to certain things that sparked our interest so we pursued them. We then learned more about them, experienced them, and perhaps became very skilled or proficient at them. This may have been a skill, hobby, or even a sport we liked to do. The more we did it, the better we became at it. However, we can all remember starting out green, as a beginner, when we may have been terrible and really had to work at it. Or perhaps we were a natural, and very gifted at it, for this quality may have run in our family line; maybe one of our grandparents was also very naturally skilled at this. In some cases we may have taken one of our innate talents and developed it further. In other cases we simply knew we were good at something and may only have worked with that gift on just rare occasions when we needed time alone to connect with ourself. And if it were some trait that we missed out on when they were being given out, we may still spend time working with it because we enjoy it even if we are not particularly good at it. In other cases when we have little to no innate skill in something, we may still work hard to develop it from nothing through lots of practice. This type of working hard has great carryover for us into other aspects of our life and helps to build our confidence that we can actually learn to do something that does not come easily.

In most cases the common denominator is having an interest or desire for wanting to do something, whether or not we are a natural at it. This can be a very powerful gift in itself: to be able to follow our heart or passion and pursue something that we have an interest in. For often there can be some obstacles or resistance to getting started with something new from both inside and outside. Some of us can get stopped at the stage of just trying to figure out where our interests lie, of being able to access our desires. In these cases, it can be a sign of being cut off from our passion for life and may need to be looked at. Often we just don't recognize what is in our own heart, for we have spent too much of our life listening to others and wanting to be like someone we are not. Something may just flow to us without any obstacles and we ignore it, because we are too busy looking for something else. For we all know that the grass can always look greener on the other side of the fence. We may need to take time out to discover what dormant seeds we have within us on our side of the fence. These may just need a little sunshine or moisture or just plain tending to them. This can be a critical part of learning to honor our gifts, since so many of them are latent or undiscovered and just waiting for us to find them.

Then as we learn to rediscover our gifts, honor, and work with them, we will become more whole and connected to ourself as part of our own healing. This will also help with healing our world. For if all six and a half billion people on the planet were exactly the same, life not only would be very boring, but our progress and development as a species would be very limited. For as we honor and develop our own unique gifts within us, we also allow them to shine forth into the world to inspire others. Nelson Mandela's 1994 inaugural speech written by Marianne Williamson well addresses this topic:

> Our deepest fear is not that we are inadequate. Our deepest fear is that we are powerful beyond measure. It is our light, not our darkness that most frightens us. We ask ourselves, "Who am I to be brilliant, gorgeous, talented, and fabulous?" Actually, who are you not to be? You are a child of God. Your playing small doesn't serve the world. There is nothing enlightened about shrinking so that other people won't feel insecure around you. We were born to make manifest the glory of God that is within us. It is not just in some of us: it's in everyone. And as we let our own light shine, we unconsciously give other people permission to do the same. As we are liberated from our own fears, our presence automatically liberates others.

9

Change & Aging
Preparing for both sudden & gradual change in life

It is a funny thing how we Homo sapiens are so resistant to change externally or socially, while at the same time we are wired for such a great degree of adaptation internally or biologically. We have talked about how we can get stuck in our ways or patterns and can be threatened by anything new or different that may disturb our status quo. We've noted how life is movement, change, and adaptation and how we need to learn to go with the flow. For when we resist change, we can be resisting life as well. For who are we that we think we have full control of everything and everyone? We certainly have seen governments that have tried to exert such control on their people, until of course the people finally wake up and collectively say no. We recall the importance of learning to say no and how those with little to no personal boundaries are much more susceptible to having others impose their will on them — be it friends, families, employers, or governments.

This comes back to looking at the difference between yin and yang. Our more internal self (yin) has more flexibility and can more easily adapt or go with the flow. Whereas our external self that is our outer more social self (yang) can be more resistant to change and adaptation. Again this is compounded by our collective outer world, culturally being more yang by nature: "This is the way it is, and you need to get with the program" or "There is my way or the highway." Many of our social institutions, be they corporate employers, organized religions, or governments, tend to tell us the rules of what we should do and what we should not do. Sometimes the short-term ramifications of standing up and saying no when we disagree can be devastating, even if in the long term the rewards are great. We therefore can become lazy, complacent, and more or less accept or buy into these outer authority (yang) dictates.

They always come packaged in such eloquent language that seems to make sense, on the surface anyway, which makes it that much easier to swallow. So we rationalize that they must be true, or maybe because we've heard them enough times we simply start to believe they're true (again, another form of brainwashing). For we all know, or at least have come to learn the hard way, that when something sounds too good to be true that it is usually not true. It may just be double-talk to confuse us. Politicians are particularly notorious for saying one thing and meaning or in fact doing the opposite. We may be told we are free and our freedom is their number-one concern, "However, we have to take away some of your civil liberties in order to protect your freedom." How stupid do they think we are? Or is the better question, how stupid are we to believe them and elect them, or did we?

So here we don't want to alienate those of us who may have a different perspective or belief, especially when talking about politics and religion. What we are really talking about is the potential situations when the inside and outside don't match up. When our outer world doesn't match with what we feel to be true in our heart. This can occur in any situation. And there have been many cases with both religion and politics, where there were not enough people questioning those whom they had put their faith in. Here are a few examples to remind us: There was the Great Inquisition in Europe during the Middle Ages when many were put to death for disagreeing with church doctrines. We had witch-hunts in the early days of America when people were burned at the stake. How was this allowed? The people put their faith in those in power and thus empowered them to do such things. What about the more recent cases of trusting our children with certain priests whom we had put our faith in? Unfortunately our faith did not seem to help our children when a number were sexually molested by these priests. In politics, let's look at the communist revolutions in both China and the former Soviet Union. The Russian and Eastern European people finally said no to the corruption of their governments. In China many millions died of starvation after the revolution because the government had the farmers turn in their metal plows and farm equipment so they could be melted down into weapons. The Chinese have not yet said no; some tried and were shot down in Tiananmen Square in 1989. All of these fatal mistakes came from the people putting their trust in their government or those in position of leadership. In the U.S. we had a second round of witch-hunting during the Cold War era, lead by Senator Joseph McCarthy. Perhaps we should take a close look at what is happening today and listen to many of our long-standing allies from Europe and other parts of the world. They think America has gone crazy since 9/11. Could this possibly be the same type of situation, but on a collective level, where our long-time friends and advisors are all asking us if we have gone mad? And our response is to simply ignore them? Is our fear reaction to 9/11 so great that we have lost much of our common sense?

The world can seem so turned around, where right can mean wrong and wrong can mean right, that we don't know whom to put our faith in anymore. It definitely is clear that we cannot believe everything we see or hear. The media try to portray the truth, but is it always the truth? The almighty dollar seems to be the only truth to many, and that which carries the most power anymore. The flow of money is now mostly controlled by a relatively few multinational corporations that seem to have a very strong influence on governments worldwide. We are told it is "to trickle down" to everyone else. Why then are more and more struggling to get by financially? These corporations have their hands in many influential pockets, including the media and many of the very leaders we have supposedly put our faith in. Do they have our freedom and best interest in mind as they pursue their tactics of globalization? *It is easy for us to believe what we want to hear and ignore that voice inside that says, "Wait a minute, something is not right here."* We can often ignore this inner voice when we are strongly motivated by fear. This can happen on the subconscious level as we are typically not consciously aware of our fear. We are quite possibly getting closer to a time of great change when we are going to desperately need to listen to that voice inside. For it is becoming more and more difficult to believe what we are told by those in control who have such a vested interest in what they are telling us.

There are actually many sources of prophecies from Nostradamus to the Hopis, Mayans, and Tibetans, as well of course as the New Testament's *Book of Revelations*, that all say similar things about these times. In short, they all reveal that there may be great turmoil of both a political and planetary (geophysical) nature causing much change, and that things will become much worse before they become better. Should these predictions prove true, are we prepared for such change? Whether or not we choose to believe in such, we can still agree that our world seems to be getting more and more challenging. And both politically and planetarily there are many things rapidly changing in our world, as it is becoming more and more volatile. It could be unwise or even perilous for us to ignore such predictions or ancient prophecies.

Again, taking the time out to go inward, self-reflect, pray, or meditate can help us to find a degree of inner calmness to balance the growing outer storm. We all know deep within our hearts and souls what is true; we just have to learn to access that truth, lest we become fanatical doing things that we may regret later. Once we have accessed our inner truth, we need to see if what we know to be true on the inside matches what we are being told on the outside. In this way we will have a better chance of meeting the many challenges of our rapidly changing world. We will be in a better position to know when to say yes and when to say no, as we allow our inner truth to guide us during times of crisis. We will better understand the flow of life and which currents we will want to flow with and which ones we may need to work with in order not to become swept away by them. In this way we can get to where we need to be. None of this is necessarily easily done, especially without first knowing ourself, our boundaries, and being better grounded.

This may help prepare us for sudden change, whether it is of a more personal nature, in our more immediate world, or be it of a more global magnitude, as certain prophecies speak of. Much of what was suggested may seem repetitive or redundant, however sometimes we need to hear things several times, or again in a different context before it starts to get through to us. This can be especially true since we are collectively so resistant to change. And yet we hate to have to kick ourself for not paying attention to something that turned out to be true *and critical for our health and well-being.* The old saying "an ounce of prevention may be worth a pound of cure" may apply should that day come when our outer world is in total chaos and we need to figure out what to do, for whatever the reason may be.

So enough on being prepared for sudden change in life. How about the more gradual change that we call aging? Are we prepared for that? And what about what comes at the end of aging or may come suddenly at any time? Are we prepared for death? Oh no, not that corpse again! Are we living our life in fear of death? Does this mean we really aren't living at all, as we are just avoiding death? Many people who have near-death experiences say that they live their lives to the fullest afterward and aren't afraid of dying. Many who are told they have only so long to live try to do the same if their body allows them to. So what keeps the rest of us who have not had such experiences from living our lives to the fullest? And why do so many of us fear getting old? Does it have to do with a fear of dying? Or maybe it's just about *how* we get old? That is, with our health and wits about us versus without such luck? *Is it just luck,* or is there something we can do about it? It may not be simply aging, but *how* we age that is the more critical factor. Or are we simply having difficulty letting go of the fact that we no longer look like we did twenty years ago? For those of us having such difficulty, perhaps we need to stop the earth from revolving around the sun every year, or figure out how to stop time. Then we won't have to deal with growing older or trying everything to not look older (as our Aussie friends like to refer to this as being like "mutton dressed as lamb"). For unless we can stop time, the fact remains that we are going to get older every year and someday die. This can be such a hard reality to face for some. However, it is what it is.

What we can change is how we relate to or deal with getting old. If we can figure out how we lose our energy as we get older, we may just be able to help reverse that process, which is not necessarily part of aging. It is entirely possible to become healthier and have more energy as we get older. In this scenario we are still aging, but we are not losing our sparkle for life and we still have our passion and energy to do things we like to do. Some of us may say this is impossible, but perhaps that is just our belief. For as long as we hold onto such a belief, then yes it will be impossible for us. In fact, we likely all know of at least one or two people who stayed young in spirit as they aged. They did not buy into any concept that they had to feel or act older as they aged. Perhaps we could say they just ripened or mellowed with age, or came into their own. Perhaps they learned to let go of unnecessary things in their life and go with the flow. Or like a fine wine, they became better with age. Wine also improves even more once it is opened and has a chance to breathe. Maybe that is the answer: *We need to be open and have a chance to breathe.*

So as we examine how we think or feel about our own aging process, we may want to ask ourself if we have learned to come to peace with *the reality of what is.* Or have we chosen to resist the inevitable truth that each year we will grow a year older and that one day we shall die? Do we believe that we are only as old as we feel? Are we willing to at least entertain the idea that we may grow older with grace and dignity, without losing our sparkle or enthusiasm for life, much less our energy? If so, then how do we go about this?

A basic understanding of energy exchange can give us a model for looking at this. "Energy in" must equal or balance with "energy out." This is like balancing our bank accounts. We can't spend more than we bring in, without having to get it from some source or another, such as a loan, which we still are responsible for paying back. Calories are a form of energy; if we take in more calories than we burn off through our normal metabolic activities or exercise, then we gain weight. It's that simple. So how have we been burning or losing our energy as we grow older? And how can we potentially prevent this? How do we stop spending more than we are making, so we don't go in debt? Or how do we stop burning more calories than we are eating so we don't get skinny? Granted, most of us can relate to this last metaphor in reverse, as far as getting fat. But it's the same with whichever metaphor we want to use; we must manage or balance our energy in with our energy out if we don't want to become depleted, tired, or depressed. With money and food it is more obvious, with our own healing life force it takes a little more to understand how this works.

Let's look at this using the model that says we have a physical body, an emotional body, a mental body, and a spiritual body. Then we can look at energy in and energy out for each of these four bodies that make up our whole. Physicality is easy to understand as that is the main operating paradigm used in our culture. On the most basic level, if we lose enough of our physical bodily fluids until we have lost a critical amount of our vital life force energy, then we die. This can be our blood or other fluids as people do die of severe dehydration. We can also, to a much lesser degree, lose energy by compensating for an illness or injury. So if we broke some bones and walk with a limp, it will take much more time and energy to walk a mile than it would without such an injury. So our compensation pattern for that injury takes energy away from us to carry out normal activities.

This can also hold true for the emotional level, as we often are still harboring some emotional wound or injury from our past that we have not let go of or healed from. This could be from any of a number of different types of emotional wounds, hurts, or traumas that we may have even consciously forgotten about and not realized we are still subconsciously holding on to. This holding on to can take a tremendous amount of our energy and we don't even realize we are doing it. Mentally we may have formulated beliefs that life is a certain way or that we need to respond to situations in a specific manner, when we actually don't. We are just hanging on to some old way of looking at the world that no longer serves us. In fact, it not only may not serve us to hold on to such beliefs, but it may take energy away from us that we could be using for a better purpose, such as to enjoy life. Spiritually we may have adapted a belief that does not serve us either, because it is not aligned with our inner truth. Supporting such beliefs that are not aligned with our truth also takes energy, like supporting a lie can take energy.

Just as we may need to stop and see from time to time where we have been spending all our money, we may also need to examine where we have been spending all our energy or vital life force. Once we are aware of where our energy is being spent in any or all of our four bodies (physical, emotional, mental, spiritual), we can then take appropriate measures. Since it often is from our past, we can stop holding on to what does not serve us, let go of it, and then go with the flow of our present life. If it is buried in our subconscious emotions, we may have to gear up and dive in to check out what lies in the depths of our murky waters waiting for the light of our consciousness. We can also re-evaluate and realign our belief systems and operating assumptions. In doing so, we will be up to date with our current reality as well as have more energy available to live and enjoy our life in the present time. So over time, from becoming more self-aware and self-examining and then learning to let go and go with the flow as we embrace change in life, we are reclaiming our own energy that had been tied-up in bad investments. In this way we can age with grace and dignity, as it is a natural process to do so, and may prevent us from having to experience the unnatural process of "dis-ease." We will then have more energy as we grow older, staying healthier and enjoying life as we are able to live it to the fullest.

10

Intention
Manifesting our heart's desire

We have looked at the four aspects of ourself: the physical, emotional, mental, and spiritual bodies, and have mostly focused on the emotional and the spiritual bodies. These four bodies or layers of our being alternate, as does most of life, in a yin and yang pattern, like alternating currents of electricity, together forming an electromagnetic field that surrounds us. The first, the physical, is a yang field and more electric in nature, while the second, the emotional, is a yin field and is more magnetic in nature, then the third, the mental, is yang and electric again like the first (the physical), while the fourth, the spiritual, is yin and magnetic again like the second (the emotional).

Thus far the focus has been on the two yin fields because the emotional and spiritual aspects of our being are more hidden and overlooked in our dominantly yang world. Just like the moon is outshone by the more obvious sun. So in our own healing process we obviously need to place our attention where there has been less focus. The emotional body is where we need to focus the most because this is the garbage dump of all our denied emotions that we don't want to look at or deal with, much less own as our own. So they are swept under the carpet, stuffed in the closet, or more accurately, they are dumped into the un/subconscious realm of our emotional body. Our spiritual body is where we need to go in order to access our own healing energy, *our vital life force*. This is our source (small "s") energy within our own being, as compared to our divine Source (capital "S"), "That Which Is Greater Than Ourself." They obviously have a relationship to one another (the two S's), but that is not the focus of this book. So remember the two beds, with the live person and the dead one. The dead one's spiritual body (small "s") was the last to vacate the premises, and that's when we could say, "no more life here."

So what about the two yang bodies? The physical again is what gets much of the focus in our yang world, but the mental actually takes all the credit. That's right, we live in a world where being up in our head is the most highly honored. However, more recently Hollywood, the fashion industry, and extensive network coverage of sports has done a good job in having the physical body give the mental body a run for its money. Actually we need to give some well-deserved credit here for this, to the sad state of our educational system. The Brits don't even think that we Yanks still speak English. They say our monosyllabic grunts and groans don't really count (*yeah, wha, huh, nah*, etc.) and they give us great praise for getting a three-syllable word out. So where is all this leading us?

The mental body is this chapter's hero, and it really is more interesting than the physical body since we already know all about the physical. For with our mental body we can create ideas, thought forms, castles in the sky, and literally send men to the moon. The mental body or mental plane, if we prefer, is also a key aspect for setting our intention or intending something into creation (again like men on the moon). The mental body would tell the physical body, "I think, therefore you are." Whereas the physical would reply to the mental, "I am, therefore you can think." Notice how these two yang bodies like competition, which is more often directed outward. Competition does not come so naturally to the two yin bodies, for it is truly a yang thing.

So let's get back to intention, or intending something into existence, or manifesting something through intention. It is truly a team effort here for we always need the spark of life, the spiritual body, to get things rolling through her inspiration. This inspiration from the yin spiritual plane steps down through the yang mental plane in the form of an inspired idea. And this is not any old idea, this is *a magnificent idea*, an elaborate and well-thought-out idea, as the mental body doesn't believe he's capable of anything less. Usually the mental body forgets to give any credit to the spiritual body for putting some spiritual fire under his butt and inspiring him on. He is actually most often quite oblivious to her existence. So now for this idea to go any farther, that is, out of the mental body's swollen head, it needs to be grounded somehow. Otherwise it could simply bounce around the mental realm forever with all the other grand and glorious ideas that don't ever manifest or come into being.

The idea cannot yet ground into the physical realm of manifestation until it has passed through the next level down, being the emotional body, which is a yin magnetic field. This can be where much can go wrong, through no fault of the emotional body, even though the mental body would say otherwise. This is because the mental body loves to blame, and he especially loves to blame the emotional body for messing up (although he has much better words for it than "messing up"). As a matter of fact our proud hero, the mental body, loves to blame because his best thought-out plans all too often don't go anywhere, *and it is always someone else's fault.* And as we said, it's usually the emotional body that he likes to blame. For she gets the brunt of the blame when things don't turn out as he planned ("very well planned, mind you"). But often enough the mental likes to spread it around, so the physical gets plenty of blame and shame as well. In fact the mental often accuses the emotional and the physical of, shall we say, "messing around" with each other when they should be working on his latest and most wonderful project. For even though he holds her in contempt and usually won't give her the time of day, he is still possessive of the emotional body when she is hanging out with the physical body (that yang competition thing again). And they do hang out quite a bit, because the physical body helps her out with her excess emotions, the ones that are more conscious that he can more easily get. Together they often laugh and play around, which really infuriates the mental body.

As we said, the mental body is most of the time oblivious to the existence of the spiritual body, so she rarely gets blamed. If he should ever attempt to blame her, she has her own way of handling such childish behavior. For instance, she may wait until the next time he goes to vainly admire himself in front of the mirror, and then she will appear in it. Her eyes, oh, they are so deep, wide open, and innocent, yet ever so full of wisdom. Looking into her eyes can be like beholding the glory of all the heavenly bodies and at the same time like falling in a black hole of empty space, they are so haunting. After such an encounter with her in the mirror, he will usually turn away mumbling something like "right . . ." as if he had just remembered something important, and then walk away like he never saw her. But for the next few days he won't be himself at all, he will be talking to himself more quietly as if he is actually listening to what he is saying for a change. He will act much more conciliatory with both the emotional and physical bodies and hardly blame them at all. They giggle and carry on in front of his back when he's like this, which of course annoys him to no end, as they know with whom he has just had an encounter. Or at least the emotional body does and she tells the physical body, but he doesn't really get it, so he just smiles his big toothy grin. Then the mental body will regain his composure and be right back to his old self by the end of the third day — if not sooner.

So let's look closer at what happens when the mental tries to move his intention down to the physical to have it manifest and it short-circuits in the emotional. The emotional, as we know, has been the dumping station for all unwanted and unconscious feelings and emotions. These are ones that may be too painful or hard to experience, too embarrassing, too sad, or even sometimes too happy, *but definitely not socially appropriate.* For they always seem to be too inconvenient at the time and simply not acceptable. She is afraid that if she let out some of these wild and happy feelings she might be seen or heard by others. She would then have to shove them back down into hiding and cover them over with embarrassment for being so socially inappropriate. Oh, and let us not forget all those buried feelings that are just too darn passionate. Yes, pure unadulterated passion for being alive or for anything for that matter. They can cause the physical to buzz and vibrate so from head to toe that he is worthless for doing anything else, and the mental can't even think straight when these feelings escape. And we can only imagine how difficult that must be for him, not to be able to think straight.

Sometimes when she is sound asleep and perhaps dreaming, some of her well-hidden feelings of passion will escape out and drift down into the realm of the physical body and up to the mental body as well. These could be passionate feelings about anything, even about something as simple as just being open and alive and breathing, just like that bottle of aged red wine. Meanwhile the mental body may be up in his head working on his latest most brilliant idea, when he is literally overrun by feelings of excitement for life, and his whole entire body starts to feel alive, not just his head.

In the old days he would wake up the physical body and they would run off together and play games or get into some type of fun-loving trouble. Back then he might be so enthralled to be feeling so much he would be inspired to write a poem about how wonderful it was to be alive, open to everything and breathing in life with great passion. He even used to acknowledge both the spiritual and the emotional bodies as being the source of both his inspiration and strong feelings of passion. For he knew that he was in a very special position having both these beautiful yin bodies on either side of him. In those old days he used to honor and acknowledge them for whom they were and their special yin gifts that they contributed from the realms of spirit and emotion. When this happened he became so well connected to himself and to them that he could also connect very well with the physical body.

When he did this he could manifest anything he wanted through the power of his intention. He knew that much of this power came from the spiritual body and was also fueled by the unchecked passion of the emotional body. And then once they all were well connected, the physical body was able to manifest anything, for it was truly a team effort. But nonetheless he felt like the star of the team being in the middle. And on some level he thought that it was mostly his yang mental body's clarity and creative intention, with the help of the yang physical body's strength and power to create, that made things manifest so well. So like the dark side of the moon being out of sight (and thus out of mind) to the brilliant rays of the sun, the spiritual and emotional bodies began to take more and more of a back seat to the over-inflated ego of the star player. He truly became more and more of a legend in his own mind. He forgot that the emotional body too sat in a key position in the middle between the two yang bodies, between him above and the physical body below. And unless he *honored, acknowledged, and connected well with her*, he could not connect with the physical body for manifesting any of his wonderfully brilliant intentions. He also forgot that these wonderfully brilliant intentions were of course inspired in the first place by the spiritual body from above.

So things continued to deteriorate as he isolated himself more and more and only acknowledged the emotional body to blame her for something. Consequently, she being lonely and sad, feeling such strong grief and abandonment from the mental body, thus became even closer to the physical body. This of course would greatly infuriate the mental body, as his possessiveness would turn into a jealous rage. But when she would confront him about it, he of course would deny such feelings. These feelings would then drop down into her emotional body and increase her burden with just another un-claimed emotion she had to carry.

The more she and the physical body connected, the more of her burdens he would take on, helping her out by embodying more and more of the emotions to which he was able to consciously relate. He would tuck them away, down in related nooks and crannies of his physical body. For instance, when the mental body came around shaming and blaming them both for all his troubles, the physical body would tuck the shame away under his tail-bone and hang his head. He would look like a dog with its tail between its legs. And when he would worry so about the emotional body and her state of distress, and about how he no longer could manifest anything like he used to, he would tuck these worries away in his belly. His gut would get all tied up in a knot and he would lose his appetite. He would alternate this with going on feed-ing binges and being worried that he might even be get-ting an ulcer, his stomach hurt him so much. So with time as the emotional body's burdens increased, his physical body deteriorated, and both of them felt miser-able being so cut off from both the mental body and spiritual body. They felt they could not connect to either anymore, since their access to the spiritual had always been through the mental body. And we all can see how disconnected from everyone he had become. They did not know that they could actually connect to the spiritual body directly, especially the emotional body, as the two yin bodies were really like sisters and could connect outside of time and space, being yin. The net result seemed to be the breakdown of the physical body who always was sick with something. The emotional body felt bad because she thought she was responsible since he had helped take on some of her burdens. However she did not know what to do about it, as she felt so terribly cut off from everyone.

This little story tells us about the power of intention and how it must flow in a connected way through the four bodies of ourself if we are going to be successful in manifesting what we want in our life. There must be a flow of energy or a connection happening between our spirit, our mind, our feelings, and our body for us to be able to successfully use intention to manifest whatever our heart desires in our life. This can be profound for us when we are able to create in our life exactly what we want or need at a given time. However if we are disconnected from our emotions, or don't want to look at something, then forget it. Also, if we get stuck up in our head and are not grounded in our body, we will not be able to manifest what we want in life. We may attract to us what we need sometimes but it may not be what we want. For we have

to be fully integrated or connected to all the parts of ourself to do so. We have to establish a good connection to
our spirit to begin with, as this is our inspiring force that
guides our mind in the right direction. For our spirit
(small "s") is also tuned in and connected on some level
with that Source (big "S"), "That Which Is Greater Than
Ourself." Our vital life force, that energy that comes
from our spirit for us to be alive and heal ourself, has its
origin in this greater Source. And remember, we agreed
that whatever different people want to call this "Source,"
that it is strictly a personal choice (so we don't need to go
start another Holy War over it).

So for this divine energy to move through us at all,
at more than just a trickle, we need to have some connection with each of our four bodies for it to flow all the
way down to our physical body. The more we work on
healing ourself and increasing our access and connection
to each of our four bodies, the better we are going to feel
in our physical body. For our physical body is the slow-
est to change, then our emotional, then our mental, as
our spiritual body is one with change and movement, or
the flow of life. Our mental body can change by simply
flipping the switch to change some belief we have been
holding on to that no longer serves us. The emotional
body can change relatively fast, but not as fast as the
mental body. There are just so many buried emotions
that must be uncovered, while at the same time not
adding any more to the heap. So the toxic cleanup crew
may be busy for a while until a critical mass is moved. In

the meantime the physical body has to patiently wait for the benefits of this trickle-down economics.

The good news is that it is not impossible and many of us have already been working hard on ourselves for a long time. So for some of us it will be a longer process and for some not so long. In either case we will know we are making good progress by seeing our power of manifesting what we desire in our life, through setting our intention, improve over time. At first we may set our intention on something and it may not manifest exactly as we want it and may take a while in coming, but with time, as we become more aligned with ourself, it will improve. We may have more pop quizzes along the way where we practice on something simple like an available parking space manifesting for us right in front of the store. Some one calling who we wanted to hear from, may be another little practice session, or money showing up just when we need it. And then we progress to the bigger things like the right job or partner, etc. For some of us, we are already well along our way with working with our intention and manifesting what we want, because that might be one of our gifts that we have learned to honor and develop over time. Whether it is or it isn't something that comes easily for us, as we learn to heal ourself, better embrace change, and become more and more connected within ourself, we will become more successful in manifesting our heart's desire through our intention.

11

Our Right Place

Standing tall in our truth with gratitude

What can happen as time passes and we have become more and more grounded and solid in our being, able to say yes or no as we need, is we start to stand tall in our truth. This can literally mean we have a bigger presence of spirit or life force in our body, and are physically standing straighter and taller. We may have old friends or acquaintances who have not seen us for a good part of a year or more remark how good we are looking or how different we look. "Did you do something to your hair?" or "Your posture looks different, you look like you are standing up straighter. Are you wearing platform shoes?" may be some of the questions we are asked. If we lived in Los Angeles, the plastic surgery capital of the world, we would be asked, "Have you had some work done?" For over time, as our spirit has taken more full ownership of our body and we have developed greater confidence in our being, we start to look different and have a bigger presence.

Much like Nelson Mandela spoke of in his inaugural address: *Your playing small doesn't serve the world. There is nothing enlightened about shrinking so that other people won't feel insecure around you.* So we have learned not to shrink and thus we seem like we have grown. People are really responding to our presence, because they feel a difference, perhaps unconsciously, as they don't remember feeling this type of energy radiating from us before. They are likely not used to this amount of light shining from most of the people they are around, since we have all culturally been programmed not to let our light shine. *And as we let our own light shine, we unconsciously give other people permission to do the same. As we are liberated from our own fears, our presence automatically liberates others.*

Standing tall in our truth may mean we are now being a beacon to others to inspire them to connect to their own truth within. And we are doing this just by being ourself, with no conscious effort. The conscious effort was in all those many, many months or perhaps years of working hard on healing ourself. For this process is not a quick fix when we think about all the changes in our life we had to go through in order to be able to stand tall in our truth. We had a lifetime worth of garbage and fallout debris we had to process and sort through one way or another. For the most part we did it on our own with the help of a few friends and advisors along the way. We learned that when it comes down to it, we are our own best advisor; we just had to get down and do some digging, excavate, and then resuscitate our advisor within.

We don't reach a sudden point where we stop and are done either. However, there comes a time where we have reached a critical mass, and our own momentum of working on our self-healing and our ability to gracefully embrace change carries us forward and it no longer seems like such hard work. It can actually seem more like fun, or play, as we embark on each new adventure of self-discovery. For each new adventure will be exciting and different as we learn to work with another gift or treasure within ourself, that we have just discovered or uncovered. This is not to say that the discovery process itself is always easy or fun at the time, as it will often be the opposite as we sort through our refuse pile. However when we think back on how we not too long ago were frozen by fear, not able to move forward, or in any direction, we now feel like we are flying in comparison, as we ride the different currents of our life. Our ability to intend something to be and have it come into manifestation gets better and better, as long as we are going with the flow of where we need to be and doing what we need to be doing in our life. Again, this does not mean there are not days or perhaps weeks where it may seem impossible to even intend ourself out of bed.

We have times when we can feel the clarity of our mind shining clearly, inspired by our spirit that is flowing down through the layers of our being through our emotions and finally into our body making us feel more alive. Again, this may not be an everyday thing we are feeling, for we may still have cycles in our life where things are not flowing. We may feel horrible as we move through yet another layer of stuff that needs to contact the healing light of our spirit. We actually can start to appreciate these cycles of healing where we know in our hearts that we are moving things that need to move or change in order for us to become more whole. We have the experience, confidence, and faith to know that we will get through this episode and come out stronger and healthier at the other end, after we have weathered the storm. Our heart begins to fill with more and more gratitude for being alive and being able to feel and experience all the depths of feelings within our being, be they pleasant or otherwise. For we can remember when we were more like that corpse on the next bed, frozen with fear, *and not able to experience or feel anything*, for we were hardly alive then.

So we have come to where we can give ourself a big pat on the back, as we breathe in with gratitude, for all that we have been through. For as we have become stronger and stronger in our whole being — physically, emotionally, mentally, and spiritually — we have truly come to appreciate many things in our life. We are appreciative for the fortitude of our spirit for staying present with us through all the good, bad, and the ugly that we have encountered along the way, ever inspiring us on.

We are thankful for our mental body for being able to find the flexibility to shift beliefs and operating paradigms, learning to go with the flow. We are grateful for our emotional body for hanging on to the burdens of all our denied and forgotten feelings, that have become our treasure chest recovered from the bottom of our sea. We are thankful for our physical body holding out, and pointing out through pain and discomfort where we need to work on ourself, and for providing the strength to carry on.

We are especially thankful that all these different aspects of ourself have been willing and able to communicate with one another, learning to once again work together as a team. And, last but not least, we are ever so grateful to our Divine Source, "That Which Is Greater Than Ourself." We are thankful for being able to feel this Divine Presence, like a bubbling spring of life, in which we can put our faith and trust that it may always sustain us. So as our own spirit becomes larger within our being, we feel a sense of, as the French would say, *largesse de esprit* within us, allowing us to be more generous of heart with others in our world.

May this serve as an example of how we may now perceive our gratitude and appreciation for the life that sustains us. Or for some of us this may simply be a gestalt of our feelings of gratefulness for being alive and for all of our blessings. *For when we can stay ever mindful and connected to a deep, heartfelt sense of gratitude, we will know our right place in the greater cycles of life, as we come to understand and appreciate that we are a part of a greater whole.* This too will help increase our connection with, and thus our trust and faith in "That Which Is Greater Than Ourself." For this connection and thus trust and faith will give us the strength and resolve to carry on as we learn to weather life's storms, embracing life's challenges with courage and grace.

Standing tall in our truth does not necessarily mean staying upright, tied to the mast as our ship heads into the eye of the storm. For this may be a foolhardy approach or even suicidal, as our ship may capsize, causing us to drown. We may need to be swept away as the waves crash across the decks of what we have always envisioned as our unsinkable vessel. This could be a relationship, marriage, friendship, work situation, or our dreams for the future, something that we thought would never capsize or sink. As we are washed over deck into the raging foam of the uncaring sea, all we may have is our faith and trust that we will make it somehow safely to shore. Making it safely to shore to be able to stand in our truth, may actually be but an illusion. For it is in that very moment as our body is swallowed by the raging swell of waves, all curled and twisted as we try to hold our breath, that we need to stand tall in our truth and keep our connection to our faith. This is the test of our faith, not worrying about the future of whether or not we make it to shore, for our salvation may come in some other form. For we may need to totally let go and give it up to "That Which Is Greater Than Ourself." We may need to do this during the height of whatever crisis we are in. The key again *is staying present in our body as we stand tall in our truth*.

Words here may not be sufficient to convey the meaning. We may need to connect to the feeling of what is behind what is being said here. We may need to put it in reference of our own experience that we can relate to, even if it is not a personal one we have had to date. For our internal reference may be more of an archetype feeling that we will then be able to access during our hour of need. This is basically a positive program for survival that is being conveyed, so we may have a template within our being to refer to on some level, if or when the waves sweep us away into the raging sea. We are simply providing our deep survival fear with an image of hope or of a positive outcome, sending it some strength and light to be there should its hour of need arrive. This will help allow us to move forward in life during those times when we feel frozen by our deep survival fear, which can otherwise become a paralyzing terror, greater than we may want to imagine.

So as we learn to better connect with both ourself and "That Which Is Greater Than Ourself," we will be learning to ride the currents of life, of which there are many. This is more of a yin, right-brain thing as well, where we simply have to follow our heart and go with what we feel to be true inside. For as we are exposed to the many currents and eddies of life, there will definitely be those that we will want to avoid and those that we will want to flow with. Learning about our right place, that center within ourself, will help us to swim tall in our truth through the many hazardous currents of life.

Another guidepost along the way, besides becoming better at setting our intention, is being able to laugh at ourself. At first it may be all too scary and serious to find any humor in our situation as we learn to embrace change in our life, or as change embraces us. But gradually we will start to be able to laugh at ourself and not take ourself so seriously. As we further loosen up, we will find we can go with the flow of those currents better and better, starting to enjoy life's sometime crazy journeys. Laughter is a key to being able to do this, and will serve us as a helpful guidepost along the way, as we observe how much we are able to laugh at ourself or our situation. So as we progress along the currents and flows of our life, can we look back at where we came from and realize that we can now laugh at ourself much more easily than before?

Standing tall in our truth with gratitude is a process. We don't all of a sudden arrive at this place. Part of our help in reaching this place, *our right place*, may even in some cases include taking certain medications that we may have needed to help get through the rough times. The key is being able to get through the rough times. However, if we are using such medications as a quick fix and a means to avoid our work, well, let's just say that our spirit may never be able to fully occupy our body. This holds true for recreational drugs as well. But if we are simply needing some temporary balance or relief from the raging storm of our life by using such, that may be fine. This is a good area to practice setting our intention. We can set our intention on manifesting the day when we can deal with our life without such help of these medications. There are, of course, a certain number of people who may need such help for the duration, due to a genetic or inherited chemical imbalance. But for the vast majority of us, such medications can keep us from getting down and going in, as they tend to disconnect us from our emotional body. It may require some good professional help during the weaning period, especially if our body has become accustomed to them, and accustomed to not feeling too much within. For feeling too much can often be what drives many to seek such medications. We always need to be as informed and educated as possible as to the benefits and risks, including what to expect during the weaning process. So, of course, we need to consult with our health professional before doing so, and perhaps receive a second or third opinion when possible. We realize that "not being able to connect with one's treasure of one's deep and buried emotions" will not be on the warning label or part of the literature as a contraindication or side effect for such medications.

We also need to remember that we cannot push the tide, as everything comes in its right time. This is part of our learning to go with the flow and to respect divine timing. So if we set our intention on manifesting total and complete healing, we may want to add "with grace" or "over a period of time." For our intention may strongly convey "right now," and if we have a lot of work to do, right now means doing all that work at once, which may mean in the hospital. So a word of warning about timing: it can be helpful to respect that all may not change overnight (not usually anyway, *but anything is possible*). After all, it took us at least our whole life of stuffing things away and making poor investments with our energy to get to where we are right now. So it may take a little time to reverse this process as well. For those of us who do not have patience as our gift, we need be careful of what we ask for. Typically with healing, the more immediate or recent layers come first. Then as we progress, we go back in time healing the older, deeper layers last. So this can also help serve as another marker for noting our progress, by seeing if we have gotten down to some of the really old, early issues yet.

As we gradually find our right place, we are aware that it comes from this feeling of deep gratitude for all life and being alive, gratitude to "That Which Is Greater Than Ourself." When we can start to feel our right place, we can also begin to access our inner strength that makes it easier to stand tall in our truth, as our spirit grows larger in our being. *We ask ourselves, "Who am I to be brilliant, gorgeous, talented, and fabulous?" Actually, who are you not to be?*

12

Parts of the Whole
Embracing our wholeness, individually & collectively

What does it mean to be whole? And if we are not whole, does it mean we are just a part? Then which part? Or a part of what? Looking at these questions from different perspectives may provide us with some helpful insights about ourself. We've talked about how we can call in more of our spirit to become present within us. So does that mean when our spirit is all present and accounted for, then we shall be whole? Becoming more whole within ourself implies that we may be gathering or collecting parts of ourself, or parts of our spirit. If we can do this, can we also discard parts that do not belong to the true wholeness of our being? Assuming this could be so, then what are these false parts about? Perhaps they are about when we are living a lie, living a life that is not truly who we are, or may not be even close to who we really are. If this is the case, then we must be a great actor, playing some role that we call our life. But is it a role we want to play for real? In other words, can we step out of it and just play ourself? Most of us have had such an experience, where we just wanted to be ourself and not play some role that does not suit us anymore. For at one time such a role may have suited us, or at least we thought it did, until we grew or changed and realized it was not who we really are.

These are all interesting concepts that may stretch some of us beyond our normal limits or to our outer limits. So for those of us being stretched, remember what we said about being open enough to understand something first, before we judge it or decide to reject it. This is as opposed to our more common knee-jerk response to something new or different, where we simply reject it without looking into it first. So let's go back to how we have been looking at being alive or being dead. In other words, we will look at the continuum, *again*, that embraces the corpse as one extreme and someone who is fully alive with their spirit present in all four of their bodies, as the other extreme. So how do we know to what degree our spirit may be present in all four of our bodies — physical, emotional, mental, and spiritual?

There are ways that we can measure the vital life force or spirit that may be occupying our being (our four bodies). There are some instruments that can do this, but they are not perfected yet. For our yang culture that believes, "If you cannot see it, it does not exist," doesn't typically fund research in such things. There are people who are gifted with inner sight who can actually see our spirit or vital life force. And it is also possible to train our hands to feel this in each of the four bodies. Those who have been trained to do so, seem to be able to independently get the same results. In other words, their findings are reproducible. Such findings also have a positive correlation with people's experience. So when someone is feeling very alive and good about themself, there is found to be a significant increase in the amount of their spirit or life force present at that time. As compared to when someone is feeling down and out, there is much less of their spirit or life force found to be present with them at that time. In this way we can use how we feel to measure how alive we may be at a given time. We can then rate where we are along the continuum between being dead and being very alive.

From the findings of those trained to feel one's vital life force, it appears that most people in our world are closer to being like that dreaded corpse than being fully alive. This may not be such a wonderful insight to have, knowing how shut down the world we live in really is. In terms of percentages using rounded figures from these findings, we could say that on the average: newborns and young children have about 40 percent of their spirit present, school age children have about 25 percent of their spirit present, teenagers have about 20 percent present, adults have about 15 percent and seniors have about 10 percent of their spirit present. The percentage of our spirit or vital life force that we have present could also translate as how alive or whole we are. So, in general, we could say that the average adult has somewhere between 10 and 15 percent of their spirit present. This figure turns out to be remarkably close to what scientists who study the brain say is how much of our brain we use. This correlation does not seem to be a coincidence. For we could say that in order to activate, use, or wake up more of our brain, we need more of our spirit to be present. Or the more of our spirit is present, the more parts of our brain we can use. In either case there seems to be a clear relationship between how much of our spirit is present and how much of our brain we are using. Does this mean that our spirit can activate our brain? Thus the more spirit we have present, the more of our brain we can have active and functioning? For there appears to be a strong correlation between intelligence and the amount of spirit present.

In fact, it is possible that there is even a correlation between the structure or grouping of our strands of DNA and how much of our spirit is present. If this could be properly researched and demonstrated to be true, we could have a way to directly measure the presence of our spirit in our physical body by looking at our DNA. The gaping chasm between the spiritual and the physical/scientific worlds would then be bridged. And that would certainly stretch some of us way beyond our normal limits, into a new paradigm of reality. Such research could pave the way for discovering how to better access not only 100 percent of our spirit, but 100 percent of the use of our brain as well. Or in short, help us to access 100 percent of our potential as human beings as we reconnect with all of the parts of ourself to become whole. As Nelson Mandela's words inspire us: *We were born to make manifest the glory of God that is within us. It is not just in some of us: it's in everyone.*

Does this then equate to accessing more of our latent gifts, talents, and skills that have been previously dormant? Perhaps this is part of our buried treasure that we need to uncover or rediscover. This may make us want to question why we are so closed down and why our world seems to shut us down, especially once we are born. Or why we are already shut down to a large degree at birth? Does this mean that we came with our spirit intact at conception and that by birth we were already a good 50 percent or so shut down? If this is true it raises further questions. For example, why do we lose approximately half of what we came into this world with at conception, during our nine months in the womb? Are we that sensitive as a developing fetus, soaking in all the trials and tribulations that our mothers are going through or may be exposed to during this period? This information seems to be painting a picture that our world is currently a very unsupportive place for us. Why is this?

If we return to the subject of becoming whole, we have thus far discussed what it might mean to be whole on a more individual level. What about collectively? It can be fascinating to see how we can affect each other both positively and negatively in regard to increasing or decreasing the amount of our spirit we have present. The last example may be a case of point. For if we are conceived to parents that have only 10 to 15 percent of their spirit or life force present, how do we suppose this may affect us during the critical nine months of development in the womb? What if we grew up in a household or neighborhood where everyone loved and cared about each other and looked out for each other? Do we think we might grow up to be loving, caring, and supportive of others as well? Or what if we grew up in a very dysfunctional household or neighborhood where there was much fear and hatred with violence and crime? Do we think we would stay fearful and hateful and be involved with violence and crime as we grew older? Studies show that this is more than likely, as these are not new concepts or scenarios to look at.

However, when we apply these scenarios to looking at how we affect each other's *presence of spirit*, it is no surprise to see how we can so easily become shut down or disconnected in order to live in this world. It is interesting to note that in the Scandinavian countries such as Sweden, we don't see such a rapid decline of the presence of spirit in newborns and young children. However since the onset of globalization where the whole world is becoming much more homogenized, Sweden and the other Scandinavian countries are no longer enjoying such a degree of isolation. And sadly as they become more like the rest of the world, this degree of strength or presence of spirit in their young ones appears to be decreasing to match the rest of the world. In China, we note that there is a sudden decline in the presence of spirit, particularly in the mental body, that comes at school age when the children are first significantly exposed to the doctrines of communism. This is particularly interesting because the senior citizens who were schooled prior to the communist revolution are actually stronger in their spirit, especially in their mental bodies, than the rest of the population (other than the preschoolers). The implication here is that the indoctrinating effect of communism is responsible for decreasing presence of spirit. Interestingly, this exact same effect can be noted with some religions when the dogma is embraced more than the core essence of the religion.

In the U.S., it is very common to see us become shut down at school age as well, but not nearly as severely as we see in China at this age, where the shutting down is so severe in the mental plane. However, this can change when Chinese people come to visit other countries such as the U.S., as then there is often seen an increase in the amount of spirit present. So the effects of homogenization can go both ways, to help increase or decrease the amount of spirit present, depending on the differences between ecosystems. And sadly it appears that many in the U.S. are becoming more and more shut down in all levels in recent years, and especially since 9/11, but also seen after the Columbine High School shooting.

So what is all of this telling us? Perhaps it is revealing to us how we can so easily affect one another, and that the lowest common denominator reigns supreme. So when someone is removed from their home environment that is relatively suppressive to their spirit, and placed in an environment that is less restrictive, they will then flourish. Or we can note an increase in their spirit. Just like if we transplant a plant or flower that is not thriving for lack of good soil, water, and sunshine to a location that is more nurturing in these lacking aspects, it will do better and thrive in its new environment. And likewise, what if we have an environment that is well suited for thriving in its relative isolation? If we then expose that environment to such toxic factors as global pollutants that are not good for healthy growth, what do we suppose will happen? Likely those healthy plants in isolation will start having similar diseases or stunted growth as those elsewhere. This analogy can be applied to the Scandinavian countries to account for the more recent decline in the exceptionally elevated presence of spirit that was previously noted in their youth. We have seen these basic biological principles in action in many plant and animal ecosystems both on land and in the sea. So why should we not think that the same would be true for us as human beings?

So where are the gardeners who are tending us? Why has there not been any conscious planning about the future of us as a species? We approach a time on this planet when what happens in one part of the world is more and more directly affecting what happens in another part of the world; where what happens to one species on this planet is more and more directly affecting the fate of the rest of the species. Where the balance of resources in one country more and more directly affects the balance of resources in all other countries. *Where the health and well being of the parts is more and more affecting the whole.*

However, in this age when globalization has very recently become an imposing reality on the planet, those forces that are directing it are corporate and market driven. That is, ruled by the desire for greater profit for a few at the expense of the many. Many of the world leaders who are calling the shots are so obviously serving the agendas of these multinational corporations, albeit clothed in the flowery rhetoric of freedom and democracy. There has become less and less distinction between their identities: those of the world leaders and the for-profit corporations, whose agenda they serve.

So spiritually speaking, it is no wonder that the whole world is so shut down and very rapidly getting worse. It has become so exceedingly difficult for our spirits to stay present in our beings from the point of conception onward. Our ability to thrive and flourish, to maintain and attain our perfection, has been derailed like a freight train loaded with valuable treasures that has jumped the tracks and plummeted down a deep abyss. More and more of us feel powerless to stop the self-perpetuating outer world steamroller of globalization that pays no more than lip service at best to the health and well-being of the planet. Nor does globalization heed the health and well-being of the earth itself or of any of its inhabitants, human or otherwise (except of course the precious few that grow wealthy beyond measure at the expense of the whole). So what would it take for this to change, to stop this heartless feeding frenzy, that feeds on the parts thus destroying the whole like a cancer? What can we do, as we may feel outwardly powerless to do anything about this? The words of Plato, in his ancient wisdom, still seem quite apt: "The cure of the part should not be attempted without treatment of the whole."

The solution is actually quite simple, it just requires our individual dedication with the full conviction and engagement of our spirit (i.e., being grounded). The solution is that *we inwardly become strong*. We learn to listen to what we know to be true deep within our being, and we stand tall in our truth as we learn to honor ourself and our gifts. We go to that place where we can connect with our inner faith and trust in "That Which Is Greater Than Ourself." We purify our temple within, physically, emotionally, and mentally to receive the full light of our own spirit. In so doing, we come to know ourself as we learn to use the power of our *own intention*. And then as more and more of us work toward our own healing and wholeness within, we will gradually reach that critical mass both within our own being, in our own healing process, as well as collectively in our outer world that reflects us. Then as one of us makes a breakthrough in our own healing, we shall be paving the way for others who are concurrently working with the same issues. Perhaps we are casting out the same demons at the same time, seemingly independent of each other. So as one of us is able to do so, it now becomes that much easier for others to do so as well. This is very similar to "the 100th monkey principle" that came from the field of psychology. It basically notes that when one monkey at a time in isolation is trained to do a difficult task, then after so many monkeys independently learn to do this, the task becomes very easy for all future monkeys to learn. This relates to the critical mass principle and to how connected all the parts are to the whole.

So as our spark of truth grows within and we find our right place, it will at first indirectly affect more and more others to do the same. Until the time comes when we shall be igniting others with more direct force by our example, as we stand tall in our truth and step forward with gratitude in our hearts. When critical mass lends power to this force, like a raging fire it shall burn away the dead debris of the unconscious greed and self-serving ways of the few. As the parts of the whole unite in a shared vision of love and caring for all, the power of greed of the few will be overtaken by the love of the many. When we can share such a vision for the future and set our intention collectively to manifest such a dream, with unwavering faith and full trust in "That Which Is Greater Than Ourself," the change shall come. We will be prepared to weather any storm, no matter how it presents itself. We need be patient in this pursuit, as our outer world likely shall continue to grow worse before enough wake up to the task at hand.

The joining together of those of us with this shared vision of love, peace, and learning to live collectively on this planet in harmony will happen individually and independently at first, as we each go inside to find our own truth. It will not matter what name we outwardly proclaim as our True Source, for It may go by many different names, for the world is made of many different people of various religions. In fact, as long as we stay polarized in any zealous belief that proclaims our own religion to be the only true religion, then we will not be able to participate in or help with the liberation of the world from its current cycle of darkness. We will actually be working against such planetary healing and wholeness, contributing to this current cycle of darkness. For ultimately we must all work together to achieve healing on such a global scale by learning to honor our differences, including our different beliefs.

The uniting of hearts shall come from within us. And it shall pass through any artificial wall of race, creed, or religious conviction. For together we must all stand naked as one, the parts of the whole. For we share a common origin, that of mankind. Bumper stickers can no longer read simply "God bless America" but rather

"God bless all of mankind." We as human beings must rise to the task of true stewardship of this planet as a whole — united as one in our hearts. When we can do this, we will have already united our individual parts within our own being, whole in body, emotion, mind, and spirit. *For the parts of the whole must first be united within each of us, within the sanctity of our own inner being, before we can hope to achieve such in our outer world.*

Notes

Notes

Notes

Notes

Notes